THE WILDLIFE MEMOIRS

About the Author

R.C. Sharma, after graduation from Poona University, was selected for Indian Forest College, Dehradun in the batch 1963-65. He topped in Wildlife Management subject and was awarded E.P. Gee's prize. After serving as Assistant Conservator of Forests for eleven years, he was promoted as Divisional Forest Officer in 1976. He was awarded I.F.S in 1983.

Also, he was trained in the first Diploma Course on Advanced Wildlife Management, form Directorate of Wildlife Research and Education (now WII), Dehradun in 1977-78. Thereafter, he served in Kanha, Bandhavgarh, Madhav, Panna and Pench National Parks of M.P. as Deputy Director and Director. Finally, he retired as Conservator of Forests from the officer of the Principal Chief Conservator of Forest (Wildlife), M.P., Bhopal 2001.

About the Editors

A.K. Bhattacharya, is an Indian Forest Service Officer of 1983, is presently an Associate Professor and Conservator of Forests in Indian Institute of Forest Management, Bhopal; and Post Doctoral in Environmental Sciences. He has contributed a large number of articles in national and international journals of repute on a range of topics related to forestry and environment. He also has to his credit a book on *Kandhar Plane Hijack,* based on his own experience as a hostage.

Dr. Bhattacharya's main contributions to the field of eco-tourism include organizing capacity building workshops and training courses for the local authorities of the various concerned departments, communities and NGOs, extending professional support to the State Government for promotion of eco-tourism, supervising research works on eco-tourism related topics, and preparing Eco-tourism Management Plans for few protected areas.

Suhas Kumar, is an Indian Forest Service Officer of 1980 batch and belongs to Madhya Pradesh cadre. Besides other assignments, he served as head of Faculty of Wildlife Education and Extension, Wildlife Institute of India, Dehradun. Presently he is posted as Chief Conservator of Forests in the office of the Principal Chief Conservator of Forests (Wildlife), M.P. Bhopal.

J.J. Dutta, joined the Forest Service in M.P. in 1948-50 batch of the Indian Forest College, Dehradun. A keen wildlifer he was chosen for Colombo Plan training in Canada in 1966. In 1977 he became Chief Wildlife Warden, M.P. and in the next six years he developed an extensive system of National Parks (11) and Sancturies (31) in the State, along with establishing an independent Wildlife Wing in the Forest Department. He was awarded the Raja Jitendra Mallik Gold Medal of the Zoological Society of India in 1982, in acknowledgement of his work in conservation of wildlife. He retired in October 1984, as Principal Chief Conservator of Forests, M.P.

THE WILDLIFE MEMOIRS
A Forester Recollects

Author

R.C. Sharma

Editors

J.J. Dutta
Suhas Kumar
A.K. Bhattacharya

CONCEPT PUBLISHING COMPANY, NEW DELHI-110059

Cataloging in Publication Data--DK
Courtesy: D.K. Agencies (P) Ltd. <docinfo@dkagencies.com>

Sharma, R. C.
The wildlife memoirs : a forester recollects / R.C. Sharma ; editors, J.J. Dutta, Suhas Kumar, A.K.Bhattacharya.
p. cm.
Memoirs of the author, retired conservator of forests from Madhya Pradesh, India.
Includes index.
ISBN 13: 9788180695179
ISBN 10: 8180695174

1. Sharma, R. C. 2. Foresters--India--Madhya Pradesh--Biography. 3. Wildlife conservationists-India--Madhya Pradesh--Biography. 4. Wildlife management--India-Madhya Pradesh. I. Dutta, J. J. II. Kumar, Suhas. III. Bhattacharya, Ajoy Kumar, 1955- IV. Title.

DDC 634.909 2 22

ISBN-13: 978-81-8069-517-9
ISBN-10: 81-8069-517-4

First Published 2008

Published and Printed by
Ashok Kumar Mittal
Concept Publishing Company,
A/15-16, Commercial Block, Mohan Garden,
New Delhi-110059 (INDIA)
Phones : 25351460, 25351794
Fax : 091-11-25357103
Email : publishing@conceptpub.com

Foreword

Stories about wild animals and their shooting in the olden days used to appear in print with some regularity over thirty years ago. With the stopping of hunting all over the country from around 1970 and 1971, these disappeared and were only obliquely referred to. The closure of hunting was to preserve game and inculcate a love for wildlife as against shooting it down. But with absence of wildlife stories and with appearance of large doses of precepts of conservation the interest of people appeared to have declined and wildlife seemed to be something for museums and National Parks and for people who had the wherewithal for visiting these.

The present volume by R.C. Sharma addresses this hiatus and in a very readable and matter-of-fact way faithfully records the personal experiences of an intrepid wildlifer among foresters. Very few people of the forest service cared to opt for this specialized branch of forestry, wherein postings were invariably in the remotest areas only and city amenities often lacking, but R.C. Sharma was one who opted for the branch of his own and stuck to it, except when ordered out due to exigencies of service.

I have been personally associated with Sharma during service and even later and have been posted up with the events by Sharma off and on. These are all true life stories showing intimate glimpses of the whole gamut of wildlife management efforts, problems and on-the-spot solutions devised by the concerned people within the framework of laws, with great devotion and application.

I am sure the book will delight its readers and create interest in wildlife and its conservation through educating its reader in the practical aspects of wildlife management. It will also answer the question of what happens to the offspring of the breeding tigers of Kanha and other such areas, who have to move out of the protected prey-rich areas.

Best wishes to the author and may he write more in his own way of his other experiences too.

J.J. Dutta

Foreword

Acknowledgements

Writing scientific papers or a book needs a skill, besides knowledge. Throughout my service, I wrote only one paper, that too in co-authorship with Dr. Kotwal, but a few articles in news papers and some scripts for Radio programmes were the only writing work of mine. Serving in the field for such a long time kept on adding to my varied experiences which became short stories of life. As and when, I used to tell these stories in my family, my nieces and my own children used to ask me to write it down. Then I came in contact with my friend Mr. Suhas Kumar (now CCF wildlife in M.P.), who on hearing some of these stories, insisted me to write them down in a book form. He kept on insisting and offered me, even to edit the same. One day I informed Mr. J.J. Dutta, our ex-PCCF & Chief Wildlife Warden also of writing such a thing. Even he agreed to check and edit it. This encouraged me a lot and then one day I started penning it down. I kept on writing pages after pages and one day I felt that I could write a lot. One day, I started typing the same myself on my computer and found that it was taking a shape. Throughout service, I had exposed a number of film rolls also, these photographs became handy to be corroborated in this book.

So, first of all I thank Mr. J.J. Dutta, who corrected and guided me in writing this small book, without whose help it would not have been possible. My heartiest thanks to Mr. Suhas Kumar also who always encouraged me and helped me not only for these stories to take a shape of book, but earlier getting me a project of conducting Wildlife Impact Assessment on M.P. roads, with Louis Berger Group Inc. (India). Mr. J.J. Dutta helped me a lot in completing that project also. It is because of these two large hearted gentlemen, that I could bring out this book. I will ever remain grateful to them both.

Here came another helping hand, Dr. A.K. Bhattacharya, the present Director, Van Vihar National Park, Bhopal, who really helped in giving the final shape to this book. His own experience of writing and publishing books was an asset in finding a publisher for this book also. My sincere thanks to him for this immense help.

Besides collecting material from my old diaries, I had to seek help from current officers in charge of Kanha, Bandhavgarh and Vanvihar, who rendred their help readily. I thank Mr. Bastaram Nagpure, Range Officer, Kisli (Kanha Tiger Reserve), Mr. U. Prakasam and Mr. Verma, the then FDPT & DDPT Bandhavgarh, Mr. L.K. Chaudhary, ex-Director Vanvihar N.P. Bhopal for their timely help in completing some important information of this book. My batch mate and colleague, Mr. K.K. Parashar also helped me a lot in completing two of the episodes in which he also appeared and kept on insisting for this book. I also thank those staff and colleague officers with whom I experienced theses incidences. I also thank my children and nieces who had sown a seed of this book in my mind. And last but not the least, I thank my wife, who remained with my children and looked after them at home when I was experiencing these incidences in the field.

Lastly, I beg for excuse from all those who have appeared in these stories and may feel hurt, I have just written down what I experienced, good or bad, without any prejudice.

Bhopal **R.C. Sharma**
6 May, 2006

Prologue

My own journey of wildlife management began when, way back in 1965, I became the winner of 'E.P. Gee prize' for wildlife management subject in Indian Forest College, Dehradun. Having been a zoology student, I had seen many animals in the laboratories, museum and during field excursions and was always curious to know more and more about these creatures of nature. The first tiger brushed aside us, when we were doing some enumeration exercise in forests of Allapally Division of Maharashtra. We were on tour from Indian Forest College and it was a summer after noon. We were spread all over in a dense Bamboo forest, it was quite shady area with a deep nala having cool flowing water. As some of us stepped on the bed of this nala, a tiger which was perhaps sleeping in this shady cool place, suddenly got up and gave a big and roar and broke through us to move into other part of the forest. Although, most of us did not see this tiger, but the roar was heard and felt by everybody, including our instructor, Mr. Vaishnav. Mr. Vaishnav never knew what exactly had happened, so he was sweating with nervousness and was trying to call all of us back, collecting and counting us. It was a good experience that increased my curiosity regarding this Royal Bengal Tiger.

For the first five years of my service in various divisions, I could never have seen a tiger, although Chitals and other herbivores were seen in Bastar, Hoshangabad and Chhindwara Divisions. I walked on the pug marks of tigers near Kotumsar in Kanger Range of East Bastar a number of times during my Range training of ten months and then while marking the coupes, at the gorge of river Sonbhadra, near Dhain in Bori Range of Hoshangabad, feeling nearness but never got a chance of seeing it. Once, a tiger killed a man in one of our coupes under marking in Jhirpa Range of Chhindwara Division and I was asked by my D.F.O. to go and inspect it and report. I asked for a jeep for this work, because going on foot or cycle or horse was quite risky. He never gave a jeep and I could not have that experience of moving in a man-eater's area (later on this tiger became a regular man-eater, operating up to Batkakhapa Range of East Chhindwara Division).

Then started the first certificate course on wildlife management at Dehradun, in 1970. I was keen to go and my D.F.O., Mr. V.K. Tiwari strongly recommended also, but I was not sent for it. Subsequently applied for three more such courses, but had to face the same fate. I had no approach and did not know whom to contact and convince except my D.F.O. About three more years passed. During this period, I was posted at Umaria and for about six months I was A.C.F. in charge, Bandhavgarh National Park along with Panpatha Range (now a Sanctuary). Got a glimpse of a tiger on a bait, while sitting on a Machan with my D.F.O. (Mr. R.K. Verma), never knowing that these tigers of Bandhavgarh will call me again and again. After promotion as D.F.O., Sales Division, Indore, could not enjoy that period of five months. On the contrary, it was a nightmare for me. Then one fine morning, received a telegram from the Chief Wildlife Warden of Madhya Pradesh, asking for the consent to go for the first Diploma course on Advanced Wildlife Management at Dehradun. Next day, I had a meeting at Bhopal, so I preferred to go in person and give my consent. To my good luck, an old friend of mine, Mr. P.K. Naik was sitting in CWLW's office as Dy. C.F. (WL). When I told him my concern, he said don't worry, even if one officer has to go for this course, it will be only R.C. Sharma. And then my train was on the track. Starting training with the most able and the devoted wildlifer, Mr. N.R. Nair as Director, Wildlife Research and Education. I enjoyed this training with other colleagues like Mr. Sukhdev and Mr. V.B. Sawarkar. Learnt for the first time the wildlife management in real sense.

After completion of the course, had the opportunity to work with Mr. J.J. Dutta at Bhopal and Mr. H.S. Panwar in Kanha. Yes! They are my first 'Gurus', under whose guidance I could learn more and more. Mr. J.J. Dutta, being our Chief Wildlife Warden and PCCF was ever inspiring for all of us, who were concerned with wildlife management.

From March 1977 to October 2001, I worked in Wildlife wing as Dy. CF (WL) at H.Q. Bhopal, Dy. Director, P.T. Kanha, Director, Bandhavgarh, Director, Madhav National Park, Shivpuri, Dy. Director (PT) Kanha (second tenure), Director, Panna National Park, Field Director, Bandhavgarh, Pench Tiger Reserve, Seoni and lastly as C.F. (W.L.) at H.Q. Bhopal. In between was out of wing for a period about six years as D.F.O., Social Forestry, Jabalpur, D.F.O, (Production), Raigarh, C.F.(Production) H.Q., C.F. Seoni Circle and Principal, Rangers College, Balaghat. During these years also, I was linked with Wildlife, whether helping in wolves menace at Barhi, guest lectures in Forest Ranger College, Jabalpur, Elephant problem at Jashpur or teaching Wildlife Management subject, regularly for three years in Forest Rangers College, Balaghat. Mentally, I was never away from Wildlife. It always fascinated me.

People were much lucky to have gone abroad much early during service. But I was luckier to have fulfilled my desire of visiting not one but two of the continents, i.e. Africa and Australia during the fag end of my service. I really enjoyed every moment that I spent in Wildlife wing and those golden moments will always cherish in my memories. I have only tried to share these moments with the readers, I am sure, they will not regret after going through these pages.

Contents

Vocabulary of Local Terms

Adivasi	: An aboriginal, tribal.
Aghan	: Ninth month of a Hindu calendar.
Ahir	: A cast, traditionally maintaining dairies and trading in milk and Ghee.
Amawas	: The fifteenth day from full moon.
Ankush	: An iron weapon used by Mahauts to control the elephants.
Ayas	: Maid-servant kept to look after children.
Bahelias	: Nomadic tribe traditionally involved in poaching activities.
Baira	: An attendant serving food and eatables in a canteen or restaurants.
Baraat	: Party consisting members of bridegroom's family and friends.
Bedies	: Iron hand cuffs worn by elephants to make them immobile.
Bidi Patta Wala	: A person who trades in Tendu leaves used in making Bidies.
Chamaar	: Cast traditionally removing skins of dead cattle and selling it to earn livelihood.
Chapaties	: Indian round bread prepared from generally wheat flour.
Chara-cutter	: Attendant of an elephant who cuts fodder for it and prepares food for the tamed elephants.
Chatai	: A floor spread prepared from thin flakes of Bamboos.
Chhatari	: A small shelter made from wooden poles and with a thatched roof.
Chhath	: Sixth day of lunar month, celebrated in Bihar as a festival.
Chivda	: Boiled, flattened and dried rice used in preparing various dishes in India and eaten raw with curd, milk or water in Bihar state.
Chowkidar	: A watchman.
Cowries	: Small sea shells used in preparing necklace and other ornaments.
Dak-bungalow	: A rest house.

Dharamshala	:	An inn for the stay of travellers.
Diwali	:	A festival of lights in India, celebrated on the day of return of lord Rama from the forest after fourteen years.
Dwitya	:	Second day of the moonlit nights.
Gathari	:	A bundle of belongings wrapped in a cloth.
Gobar	:	Cowdung.
Goondas	:	Ruffians.
Gujaraties	:	People belonging to the state of Gujarat.
Guru	:	A teachers.
Hanka	:	A beat or drive conducted in the forest in order to bring out animals.
Hauda	:	Generally a wooden seat fixed on elephant's back to sit on.
Jaggery	:	Concentrated and dried sugar-cane juice also known as gur.
Jhoolaghar	:	A centre of various types of swings for children.
Kaandi	:	A type of corn on the foot soles of elephants.
Kacha	:	Made of mud and raw bricks.
Kartik-poornima	:	Full moon day, falling after Diwali, generally during the month of December.
Kauri-likhai	:	A commission fixed for writing a cash receipt.
Khasra	:	Patwari's village papers showing various units of land.
Khatka	:	A small door made of wood or bamboos without hinges or bolts.
Khichari	:	A festival celebrated in Bihar State during the month of January.
Kirtan	:	Chanting of God's name, singly or in groups.
Kothi	:	Old bungalows with big courtyards around it.
Kumra	:	Gourd.
Kumra band	;	Gourd like.
Laddoos	:	Sweet generally made of gram flour, in the shape of small rounded balls.
Machan	:	A hide on a tree.
Mahaut	:	A person who commands and drives an elephant.
Mahua	:	Flowers of tree, *Madhuca latifolia*, used as food and also to prepare local country liquor.
Majmuli map	:	Map of a village or town, showing physical features but not contours.
Marg	:	A road.
Mataki	:	A small earthen pot used to preserve country liquor.
Maund	:	An obsolete Indian weight measurement approximately equal to one Kilogram.
Mela	:	A fair.

Mela shikar : A method of capturing wild elephants, in which you enter the herd of wild elephants on the backs of tamed elephants known as 'Kunkies', then put noose in the neck of small calves, scare away the mothers and other elephants, then virtually snatch these calves and bring them to the training camps.
Mrigaband : A thin and lean elephant looking like a deer.
Naka : A forest guard's post or H.Q.
Nala : A small rivulet or a drain.
Nautanki : Plays enacted with a lot of loud music, where spectators freely pass comments and talk to the actors during the plays.
Netas : Local leaders.
Praat : A big plate, generally of brass, used to dough the flour.
Parad : A community hunting by the tribals, still prevalent in many parts of the forest.
Patangas : Flying insects which come out in swarms, just after rains.
Peehari : Local edible mushrooms growing on the forest floor.
Phagun : A month of Hindu calendar, corresponding to middle of March to middle of April approximately.
Pharsa : A weapon with sharp and wide blade.
Poha : Same as chivda.
Pooja : Worship.
Poos : A month of Hindu calendar, corresponding to middle of December to Middle of January approximately.
Ramkatha : Story of Hindu epic Ramayan.
Ramlila : Enacting the story of Ramayan.
Saar : A room, where cattle are kept during night.
Saari : A long cloth, generally five metres in length wrapped by women around waist and legs in India.
Sangam : A junction or confluence of two rivers.
Sarpanch : A head of the local village body.
Shikari : A local hunter.
Shivratri : A religious festival celebrated for Lord Shiva.
Soordas : A Hindu religious poet of medieval period who was blind.
Sutali : A thin rope made of jute fibres.
Sutali bomb : A cracker made and wrapped in Sutali, making loud noise.
Takhat : A bed made of wooden planks.
Tatta : A partition made of bamboo flakes, woven in a rectangular shape.
Tola : A small part of a village, consisting of a few huts only.
Tonga : A horse-cart to carry men and the luggage.
Vishwakarma : In India, god of engineering.

Episode-I

The Man Eater of Bandhavgarh

It was evening of 19th December, 1981 and time was around 4.30 p.m. I was on my way to Tala (the tourist and the Range H.Q. of Bandhavgarh National Park), where I was to attend the Commissioner of Rewa, who was reaching Bandhavgarh that evening. As soon as I reached Koluabah, a roadside hamlet (a tola of village Garhpuri), just three kilometers before Tala, I saw our park elephant Gautam with four women tourists coming on from Tala side. It was a strange sight for me, because firstly the road was outside the park, secondly, tourists were taken inside the forest for a ride and not on the road. I stopped the elephant and asked the *Mahaut* Nair the reason for this diversion. He said that a woman was killed by a tiger near Koluabah and he was taking these tourists to that spot to show them the tiger. It was foolish on his part, taking tourists to such a site. I made the elephant sit, asked all those women to sit in my jeep and brought them back to the forest rest house, Tala. I had sent that elephant to the spot and asked the *mahaut* to wait for me. I came back to Tala also to fetch a rifle or a gun from Range office and of course to drop the tourists back. As the Range Officer and my Assistant Director both were not at Tala that moment, I could not get any weapon for self-defence.

When I reached back at Koluabah, the dead body of the victim by name Manitia Bai (an old lady of about sixty years age) was already brought back from the forest, by her husband, her son, villagers and the forest department staff. I may clarify here that this P.W.D road from Umaria to Tala used to form the boundary of Bandhavgarh National Park that time, hence, this site of killing and the village hamlet were just on the fringes of the park and practically speaking, it was under the control of the territorial D.F.O. Umaria. Therefore, S.D.O. Shri R.K. Sinha was already present with his staff. Only one thigh was completely eaten by the tiger. My Range Officer Mr. Ashutosh Dubey was also present there, along with two more elephants. They had all gathered on the outskirts of the village at the foothill of a small hillock. As was told by the husband of that deceased woman (Mohan Baiga of Koluabah), that they were grazing two goats, two-three cows and their calves on the lower slopes of that hillock. The old man was sitting near a stump, whereas his wife was cutting leaves of some small trees to feed the goats and was on higher side, towards the forest, the time was around 2.00 p.m. Suddenly a huge tiger appeared from behind the bamboo clump and rushed to catch a goat. The goat had seen it charging on, so it ran as fast as possible down the slope and could escape the attack. During this attack, the tiger virtually brushed aside the old woman, who was busy cutting the leaves. Seeing this attacking tiger so close, she fainted and fell on the ground. As the tiger turned around to go back to the forest, it picked up this hapless old woman in its jaws and started moving towards the forest, uphill side. Her husband, who was seeing this all was stunned. He tried to shoo off the tiger by shouting and hitting the ground with the axe he had in his hand also. But the tiger did not leave his wife and moved towards the top of the hillock, known as Banderchui. Later on he reached the village, called his son and others and told them every, thing. They all got together, collected some sticks and axes and went after the tiger, but could not save the old woman.

By the time they could locate the tiger, the woman was already dead. On hearing the shouts of so many people, the tiger left the dead body and moved off to the bushes. The left thigh of the dead body was completely eaten by the tiger. The husband and other villagers immediately wrapped the body in a sheet and brought it down. When I reached there, I inspected the spot along with the husband of that woman, where the tiger had really charged the goat and this entire episode had taken place. The sun was about to set now, so I was planning to follow the tiger next morning. It was not safe to follow a man-killing tiger in the dark.

But then our mahaut, Nair started insisting to take me to the spot from where these people had recovered the body (where the tiger had actually eaten the body). I was reluctant, because I had no weapon with me and secondly, the dead body was also with us now. But then on insistence of Nair, other mahauts and the husband of the deceased woman, I yielded. They assured me that we would return before it was dark. Mr. R.K. Sinha, S.D.O. and Ashutosh Dubey, my Range Officer sat on one of the elephants, on the second elephant were her husband Mohan and her son Daddi and I was occupying Gautam, the elephant with Nair as our great mahaut.

Actually this area was an old abandoned coupe of Bamboo forest. Bamboo had grown so dense that even elephants were finding it difficult to move through it. They actually had to open the clumps with the help of their trunks, bring down culms with the feet and then move up the hill, a very tedious, slow and dangerous process. Anyhow, we could reach the hill top in one and half hours time, contrary to the estimation of my guides who thought that the total time required for up and down journey was just half an hour.

The spot from where the dead body was lifted had a small piece of *saari* of the ill fated woman and a stain of blood. It was a small, flat and grassy patch. This patch of land was open from the top but surrounded by tall bamboos on all sides. Due to this reason, when we reached there, it appeared very dark as if the sun had already set. This is the right time for any normal tiger to move around in the forest. I was a little scared now. I called everybody near me and warned them that the tiger must be around that area only and also in a bad temper (having lost its kill). So everybody was asked to keep his eyes wide open so as to locate the tiger on its first sight and move back fast to the village, so that we were clear of that dense bamboo patch at the earliest. Evidently it was a danger zone.

There on the top we could see an old extraction path, a longer route, but certainly easier for the elephants to walk on. I asked the other elephants tc lead, and mine was the last. I sat facing back, with crossed legs on the *hauda*, so that I could see any movement behind us. As said earlier, we had nothing for our self-protection, not even a stick. It was already dark. The extraction path was a zigzag one but was easily visible. Now we were moving much faster. After second turn, suddenly, I saw a long figure following my elephant. My heart stopped for a moment. The tigers may not attack an elephant from front side, but certainly are not much intimidated by the back of an elephant. It was a huge and a very long tiger and certainly not a normal tiger. A normal tiger avoids human movement and usually changes its route on hearing human voice. But this tiger was following us brazenly on the heels of our elephant. I lost no time in deciding that this was the same tiger, which lifted and ate that ill fated woman. I asked Nair to turn my elephant immediately, and gestured occupants of other elephants to stop wherever they were standing. This was the first time I was repenting my decision to have yielded to Nair's foolhardiness. When you are pursued by a grown up and bold tiger the elephant back is not a safe perch. If an enraged tiger decides to jump over it, he can very easily do so.

Now when the elephants turn to face the tiger, the tiger also stopped on the extraction path where it was. It opened its mouth wide in rage and growled, certainly in a very bad mood. I asked Nair to move one step towards the tiger, just to scare it away. And there was this determined Royal Bengal Tiger who budged not an inch, again a big growl and a wide open mouth. This was the time my mahaut Nair also lost his nerves. He asked me what to do then. I was cursing him and my luck. I was afraid that if any further accident/attack took place that evening, I will have to own the responsibility and might even lose my job. But then I had to face this situation and find out some solution. We had to crush the courage of the tiger; otherwise it was determined to crush our bones. I asked Nair to move two steps and also fast; towards the tiger (luckily our elephant Gautam was also very brave). But this tiger wouldn't budge an inch, instead it sat there twisting its tail and growling in anger.

Fig. 1.1: Daddi, The Son of First Victim Manitiabai

Fig. 1.2: Spot Where Tiger Lifted Manitiabai

In whole my service, then of twenty years, I had never seen such a sight. Only good sense did never leave my mind and I kept on thinking the ways to defeat this potential man-eater. I called other two elephants also near ours. Now was the last attempt. Now or never. I kept my elephant in the centre and the other two on either side, a pointed three-faced simultaneous attack on the tiger. As our three elephants moved fast towards the tiger, it felt confused for the first time, got up and ran towards the bamboo clumps. Yes! There I won for the first time in half an hour of high drama in the forest. The 'terror', which was visible to us, had vanished in the forest; how far we never knew. The question now was that if this bad tempered tiger, which might reappear out of any roadside bush, whom will it attack and with what result? If anyone of the elephants lost its cool and bolted out of fear throwing off somebody from the back of the elephant what would happen. I remembered God a number of times and promised not to commit such foolishness in future. The only strategy left to us now was to shout loudly, make sounds on the 'hauda' rods by hitting the '*ankush*' on it and move fast out of this thick bamboo forest. Once again two elephants were leading us, myself the last in the row, facing backwards in the same position. Thank God this time it did not follow us so close, though it was certainly coming after us at a safe distance (confirmed from the alarm calls of barking deer, right behind us). At last we came back safely by about 7.30 p.m. The dead woman's body was brought to her house by that time, to be cremated the next day. The tiger kept on moving around the hut all through the night (the huts in such '*tolas*' are located singly and far apart).

I came back to Tala. This was an experience of my life, facing a man-eater (empty handed) on its first human kill. This tiger, subsequently killed four more persons and took around eleven months time when it was finally shot dead by my successor, Mr. S.M. Hasan on 21-11-1982 on Sulkuni nala near Garhpuri. The second kill also took place during my period in Bandhavgarh. It was one morning of 19th April, 1982, I was returning from Tala at about 11.00 a.m. a man came on cycle from the same village Koluabah. Obviously, he was very panicky and informed me that a man called Khairauha (Budhuwa) baiga was killed by a tiger right on the fringes of their village. It happened so that when he and his wife were returning home after collecting Mahua from the forest, his wife saw a *tendu* tree on the outskirts of their village. She asked her husband to collect some ripe fruits, which had fallen on the ground, for their children who were hungry at home. When Khairauha (Budhuwa) was picking up fruits from the ground, his wife was looking at him and then suddenly the tiger, which was perhaps lying under, some trees ahead of them came rushing at him, gave a big blow by his fore paw that broke his neck. For a moment his wife was frozen with fear, then realizing the fact started shouting at her loudest. A few more persons gathered and the tiger left its victim and ran to the adjoining forest. It could not eat any part of this poor man.

Fig. 1.3: The Man Eater's Dead Body, Showing Clear Wound on the Nostrils

I went back to Tala, picked up my rifle this time and came to the spot. Mr. Dom Moraes, a journalist from Bombay was also there at Tala, and accompanied me to the spot. (Later on he wrote an article in the *Illustrated Weekly of India*). In this episode, the tiger was sleeping in the nearby nala and was disturbed by the movement of Khairauha on dry leaves, who was kneeling down to pick up tendu fruits. Perhaps it mistook him as some quadruped animal grazing and attacked him. After this second kill, although we were not yet sure of this tiger having become a man-eater, we were still cautious about its activities. In the first case, it had never charged that Manitia Bai, she herself fainted and fell down after seeing a tiger so close. In the second one, it only hit the man with its fore paw and never ate any part of his dead body. So the report was sent accordingly.

I left Bandhavgarh on 05-07-1982, on transfer as Director Madhav National Park, Shivpuri. So the rest of the story is as told by Mr. S.M. Hasan, my successor in Bandhavgarh and Mr. J.J. Dutta, the then Chief Wild Life Warden, M.P.

Once again a grazier of Garhpuri village was killed on 14-07-82, while he was grazing his cattle in the forest. This was after a gap of almost two and a half months time. Mr. Hasan immediately rushed to the spot and inspected the carcass. The victim had only three canine marks on his neck. The left lower canine was missing. Mr. Hasan tried to search for the tiger, but could not find it. In course of enquiry he could find that this tiger was moving around Ranchha, Dobha, Garhpuri and Bagaiha villages. People were quite panicky and non-co-operative. They were only criticizing the department and officers. Hasan immediately informed the Chief Wildlife Warden and requested him to declare this tiger as a man-eater.

Mr. J.J. Dutta, the then C.W.L.W. came to Bandhavgarh on 28-8-82, also came Mr. Martand Singh, The ex-Maharaja of Rewa. Mr. Dutta moved from one village to another collecting evidences and ascertaining the identification marks of this tiger, so that an innocent tiger was not killed instead of the real culprit. Monsoon was on its peak, so the movement of vehicles was difficult in the operational area of the man-eater. Mr. Dutta decided to establish a camp in a deserted forest guard quarter at Bagaiha to have an easy and fast approach in case of any event. He stayed there for ten days time, during which he came across one man by named Kulla Ahir of Bamera village. He had very poor sight (almost blind). One day, when he was grazing his cattle in the forest near Bamera, this tiger charged him. He could only see this huge figure of tiger, which caught him from his shoulder. The cattle bolted here and there. Then this grazier Kulla fell flat on the chest, his turban was thrown out. Now the tiger caught hold of his head from the backside. On seeing this, one of his faithful bull-ox came rushing for his rescue, gave a big blow to the tiger with his horns, almost throwing him away. The tiger left the man and ran away. This man Kulla was also having only three canine marks, clearly visible on his head.

Mr. Dutta was quite convinced. Though he could not see the culprit during his stay, but he could gather information regarding its pugmark also. The fourth or the smallest toe on its right forepaw was not in a normal position. It was pushed upwards. An abnormality, which might have been caused due to an injury, sustained while fighting with other tigers or otherwise. So giving these clues to identify the right tiger, Mr. Dutta authorized Mr. Martand Singh and Mr. Hasan to shoot this tiger and came back to Bhopal.

Mr. Martand Singh put his local shikaries, Gullu and Sukhdas to search for the man-eater. On 27-9-82, a cow was killed near Garhpuri by the same tiger. The local staff of Mr. Martand Singh identified the tiger, informed him accordingly and tied another bait (a buffalo) to localize the same. In turn, Mr. Martand Singh asked them to erect a '*Machan*' near the kill site. When Hasan came to know about it, he also wanted to see the tiger from the elephant back, but they stopped him lest the tiger would have left the site due to disturbance. Mr. Hasan asked Mr. Martand Singh to shoot the tiger from the back of Gautam elephant, but he declined it. He preferred to shoot it from '*Machan*' only, with a '*Hanka*' or a beat. Then Hasan offered to keep the elephants in front of the beaters so that this man-eater caught none of the beaters. Certainly, it was not proper to conduct a beat for a man-eating tiger. Any way, nothing came out of this beat as the tiger had already left that area.

On 10th October, 1982, two graziers, Phoolchand and Shankar ahirs of Garhpuri were grazing their cattle near Bhadrashila area. Phoolchand was walking ahead of Shankar. Suddenly they heard alarm call of Chitals and could sense a tiger nearby. They preferred to take their cattle back home, but could not see the tiger, which was already stalking them. After a few minutes, when Phoolchand turned around, he saw that the tiger was carrying Shankar away by holding his left cheek and jaw. Phoolchand came running, flashing his axe in an attempt to save his friend. But this tiger now left Shankar and caught Phoolchand from his neck and dragged him to a nearby nala. During all this episode other villagers also gathered and followed the tiger, but could not save Phoolchand, who was dead by that time and the tiger had already left the spot. Shankar was immediately rushed to Umaria hospital, where he also succumbed to his injuries during that night.

On 16th October, 1982, a cow was again killed near village Ranchha. A 'Machan' was erected and Mr. Martand Singh conducted a 'Hanka' or a beat on the third day. Again it was unsuccessful. On 19th October, 1982, this tiger chased a grazier near Bhadrashila on P.W.D. road, when suddenly a truck arrived there. As driver raised the engine of the truck, tiger abandoned the chase and ran back to the forest. Fortunately, this grazier was saved. The Park staff identified this tiger from its pugmarks.

On 21st October, when Hasan came to Garhpuri for a routine enquiry about any kill by this tiger, then only he could know that this tiger had killed a buffalo on 20th i.e. a day earlier, near Garhpuri on Garhpuri–Bagaiha forest road. After a lot of persuasion the grazier agreed to show him the kill. Hasan took him along on his elephant and on way could see the clear pug marks of our man eater. He had only one elephant Gautam with him. When he inspected the kill, the tiger was not there. He looked around for the tiger which was sitting a little away from it. Hasan could see clearly, the wound on his nostrils that was washed fresh due to the rain. Out of tension a lot of adrenalin was being pumped into his system. He was very eager to have a shot at it. But the mahaut Nair was reluctant to take any risk with single elephant. When they were still planning, other two elephants also arrived. Earlier Hasan and the Forest Ranger occupied the same elephant with back-to-back and facing in the opposite directions. In such position it is very difficult for both to aim one object and shoot simultaneously. Now the Ranger took position on other elephant. In the mean time, the tiger also came back on the kill and started eating it. Hasan took his elephants with a wider circle and positioning them on the backside of tiger. Hasan asked the Forest Ranger to load both of the barrels of his twelve bore gun and only to shoot a cover shot, if Hasan's bullet hit the tiger first. Hasan aimed at the nape of the tiger and started waiting for the tiger to lift the head. It was a pin drop silence, only heart beat (obviously high) was audible.

At this position, there was a 30' wide nala in between the elephants and the tiger, known as Sulkunhi nala. The moment tiger lifted its head; Hasan took a shot with his .315 rifle. It hit the target perfectly. The tiger threw its head in front and then Forest Ranger emptied both of the barrels of his gun. The tiger was still writhing with pain. After Ranger's shot, it got up on its legs when Hasan took another shot at the thigh region. Now it turned over and fell in the nala. Due to dense and tall grass in nala, it was not visible but was still struggling and gasping. After moving the elephants further on a suitable position, they could see the tiger and then Hasan emptied the magazine

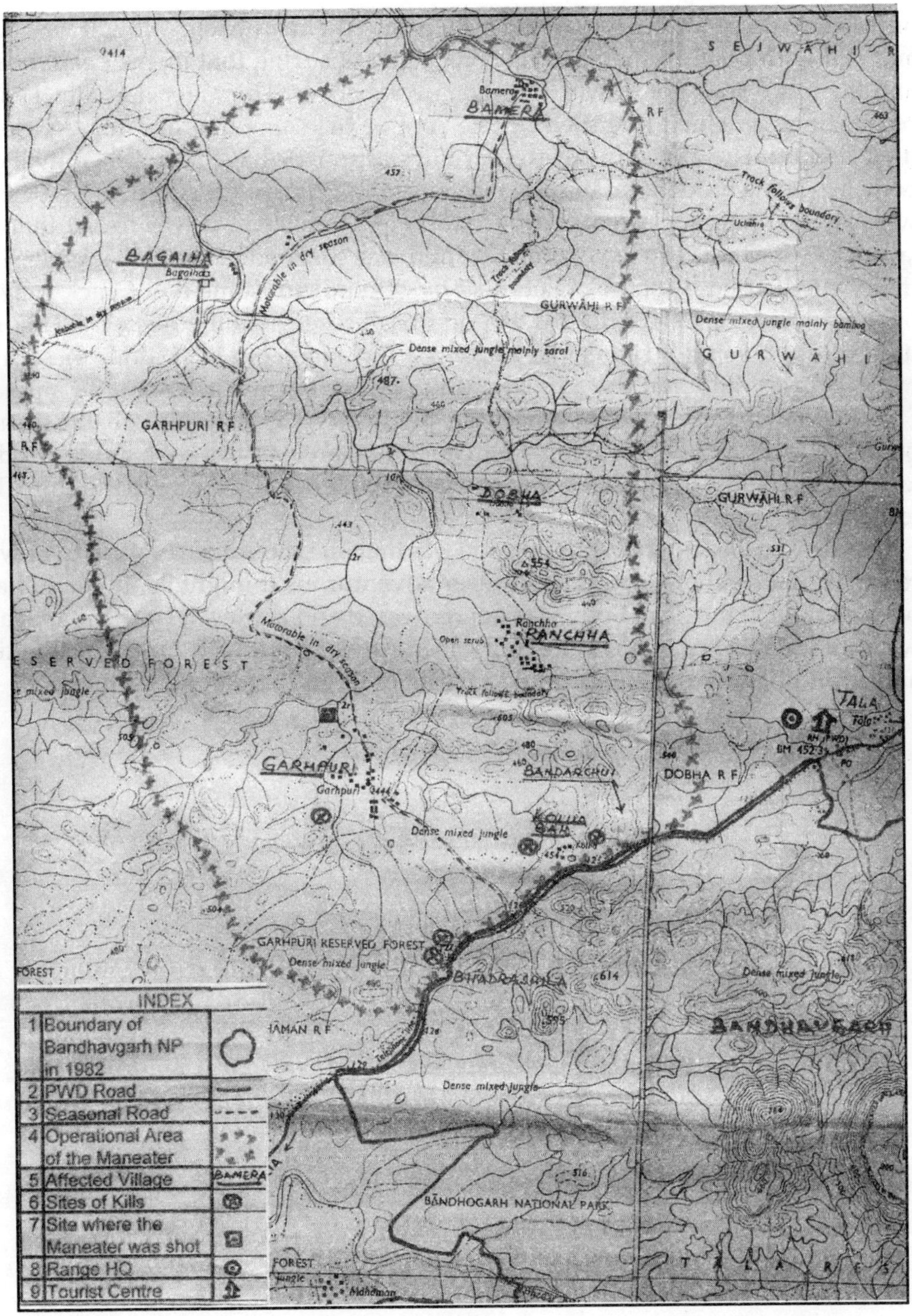

Fig. 1.4: Map Showing Area of Operation of Man-eater of Bandhavgarh

of the rifle, firing all the remaining bullets into the man-eater. Now it was dead and still with no movements in its body. After ensuring that it was dead, Hasan and the other staff got down. The menace was over. This tiger had attacked 18 persons out of which five died on the spot or the same day and three persons died later on. The gun shots were heard in Garhpuri village also. When the dead body was being brought to Tala, the villagers in Garhpuri were singing and dancing with joy and happiness. Later on, from the post-mortem, it was found that the jaw of the tiger was broken on one side and was suspended on the backside. This injury was caused by some pellets shot by 12 bore gun some times back, may be by some poachers. Externally, the wound was fibrosed. Another pellet had injured its nostrils, causing a finger deep wound with maggots in it. Both these man made injuries rendered the animal unfit to kill its normal prey of wild animals. Still it was in a perfect health otherwise, but how. As Hasan told me this tiger of ours was in a habit of following a female of that area and as soon as she used to kill an animal, this tiger used either to share it with her or even grab the entire kill for himself.

The lesson I learnt from this episode was that one should never yield to unwise requests of the subordinates, howsoever adventurous it might be. It would have been all right; if the dead body was not recovered and retrieved from the spot and we were suitably armed to protect ourselves. Anyway, our luck and quick thinking and application of experience could save all of us on that fateful evening.

Episode-II

Baghdalaka Cave of Bandhavgarh

It was mid-May of 1980, and time was around 11.30 a.m. Myself and my Assistant Director, Shri G.D. Dwivedi were sitting in the Forest Rest House, Tala of Bandhavgarh National Park. We were discussing certain issues, and then I enquired from Dwivedi, whether he had seen the 'Baghdalaka cave' of the park or not. He had been working in the park as Assistant. Director for almost two years then and had not seen this cave. I was annoyed a bit as these youngsters were not much interested in seeing the forest or the wildlife. In the meantime, another A.C.F., Mr. R.N. Dubey joined us. Mr. Dubey was working as Superintendent of Sitanadi Sanctuary, Raipur and actually belonged to a small town of Manpur near Tala. He had come on leave. Even he had worked in Bandhavgarh as Assistant Director for two years before Shri G.D. Dwivedi. Earlier in 1978, he accompanied me during the survey of the Wild Buffaloes habitat in now Udanti Sanctuary of Raipur. He was very happy to meet me again and asked me whether many tigers were being seen in Bandhavgarh. I nodded in affirmative and said "Yes! But first tell me whether you have seen this Baghdalaka cave or not". Even he was unaware of it.

Immediately, I asked them to accompany me, because I wanted to show them this cave. They came with me. We had to reach the "Sher Marg", an interior forest road to reach the cave that was about thirty kilometres away from Tala. After about 45 minutes drive, we left our jeep on the Sher Marg and started walking towards the cave. Our driver, Mohan was also coming for the first time to see this cave and was equally enthusiastic about it. We all were walking fast on the descending rocks and Mohan was in the lead, it was about 12.30 p.m., a very hot summer. Accidentally, a stone got hit by Mohan's foot and rolled towards the cave. A slope from opposite side met the slope near the cave over which we were walking. Mohan was standing almost on the edge of the vertical drop of about 6 feet in front of the cave. We were just behind Mohan, keeping a distance of about 5-6 feet between each of us. As the

Fig. 2.1: Baghdalaka Cave of Bandhavgarh

Fig. 2.2: Slopes where the Pair of Tigers Moved after Showing up Near Baghdalaka Cave

stone rolled and fell near the cave with a thud, a pair of huge tigers came out of this cave, growling in anger. They climbed up our slope and were standing in front of us, at hardly a distance of 5-10 feet, a hand shake distance. We all were glued to the spot, wherever we were standing. Though, the breathing of all four of us almost stopped but that of the tigers was so loud and clear. Mohan was the nearest one, and then myself, Dwivedi and Dubey. In whisper I cautioned each one of them, not to move an inch. Just stay put and keep your eyes on the tigers, I had never seen tigers so big and so close on foot and that too in so much anger. Both tigers were staring at us, so were we. For about two minutes they were growling like that, and once they appraised our harmless intent they turned around and started climbing the opposite slope. Intermittently, they looked back at us. Ultimately, when they vanished into the woods only then we started breathing once again. For a few moments we could not talk to each other. Then there was a broad smile on everybody's face. Perhaps all were thanking their stars. Now Mohan picked up another stone and threw it towards the cave, to ascertain the presence of another pair of tiger if any. I told him that tigers do not live in herds like deer or the pride of lions, so there was nothing to worry about. We quickly got down into the cave, saw the resting place of tigers and got out. We came to our jeep, evidently quite fast and returned to Tala. Now when I asked Dubey if he wanted to see our tigress with four cubs near Chorbahra nala, he replied in negative, saying *"aapne to abhi sher se khawa diya-tha"* (just a few moments ago you had almost offered me as food to the tigers) and that evening he vanished from Tala, like those tigers did a few minutes earlier.

In such situations, one should never lose nerve. The tiger is basically a 'gentleman' and usually never attacks a human being unnecessarily. The human movement at such a close distance puts them in fear of being attacked and then they charge in self-defence only. They never charge an aware prey, when it is looking at the tiger; usually it prefers an unaware animal. So when so close, do not move your eyes from the tigers and do not try to run away, because a man stands no chance before a tiger. Let the tiger be sure of your harmlessness and then it will certainly walk away on its own course.

The importance of this cave is, that way back in 1973, when my senior colleague Mr. Ashok Masih and I were conducting wildlife population estimation exercise in Bandhavgarh National Park, an old villager of the then "Bathan village" told us about this cave. As he said, in the olden days there used to be some sages who used to live in this cave and also used to keep some tigers with them tied with chains. We had seen this cave that very day only. Then another peculiarity about this cave is that on the rock of this cave, a number of 'pug marks like impressions' of various sizes are there. As if fossilized pug marks are there. We had a long discussion with Mr. Wahid Khan, the then Conservator of Forest, Shahdol circle, on the possibility of these being real pug marks of tigers or not. Well, this mystery is still there. Whatever it may be, this is certain that tigers do like this cave and do take shelter in it, this being the most suitable place in this part of the park.

Episode-III

Death of a Brave Wildlifer

I never believed in astrology or the horoscope, but one incidence in my life made me believe in this science. We were having Wildlife training at the Directorate of Wildlife Research and Education Dehradun (now Wildlife Institute of India). Our Director, Mr. N.R. Nair was the only faculty member during our first batch of Diploma course. We were to go on South India tour to Karnataka, Tamil Nadu and Kerala. Mrs. N.R. Nair called our fellow trainee from Kerala (Mr. Surendra Nath Asari) and told him that Mr. Nair's stars were not favourable those days, so she was not willing to let him go on tour, but there was no alternative, he was the lone instructor in the Directorate and ours was the first batch. So reluctantly she permitted him to go, with an advice to us that Mr. Nair was not to be left alone in the forest at any time. All of us were supposed to accompany him, whenever he went to the forest.

We engaged our taxies from Coimbatore and started for Bandipur sanctuary (now a Tiger reserve), near Mysore in Karnataka. We reached Bandipur at about 5.00 p.m., but we were astonished to see that no officer from the Karnataka Forest Department was there to receive the class. They had confirmed our tour programme, but somehow no body was deputed to conduct our tour in the sanctuary. At the reception counter, only a Deputy Ranger was present, who could neither speak, nor understand English or Hindi. It was difficult to communicate with him. Mr. Nair was very much annoyed and asked us not to unload the taxies. He said, he would take us to Kerala State instead and complete the programme. We were asked to turn the taxies again towards Coimbatore. Then he said "let us have a cup of tea or coffee, in those roadside tea-stalls, before we again go back to Coimbatore". We were taking tea individually, in the tea-stall of our own choice. And then Mr. Nair met Mr. A.J.T. John Singh (now Addl. Director, WII), who was doing his research on wild dogs (Cuon alpinus) in Bandipur sanctuary, from

Madurai University. He, while talking to Mr. Nair, impressed him very much with his work. Mr. Nair asked him if he could take the trainees of our batch with him in the field, to show us how he was collecting various data in the field. Mr. John Singh agreed to take 2-3 trainees at a time along with him, as he used to go on foot and a crowd could disturb the animals.

The destiny again changed the mind of Mr. Nair. He said "there is no dearth of accommodation at Bandipur, as the dormitory is available for the trainees and a cabin for me. Now I have decided to stay back here only, so that we can accompany Mr. John Singh in small batches and learn the actual fieldwork/exercise in 2-3 days time". That is how the programme was again changed and we unloaded our luggage from the taxies and settled down in the dormitory. Nobody was aware what destiny had in store for Mr. Nair in other three days time.

Next day, as Mr. Sukhdev (now P.C.C.F in Tamil Nadu) and I were returning from the field, Mr. Nair stopped us in front of his cabin and called us. He said that Mr. John Singh was very much afraid of the wild elephants. He said that John Singh needed not to be scared of these elephants, as an elephant is otherwise a very gentle animal. It never attacks human beings unnecessarily. He enquired from Mr. Sukhdev also, his experience about wild elephants. Mr. Nair had worked in Elephant country in his state for many years and he was of the opinion, that elephants, even if they charged, the first charge was usually a 'mock charge' and before a final charge a man had sufficient time to escape. He was keen to remove this fear from the mind of Mr. John Singh. I could not say anything, as I had never seen wild elephants in M.P. Any way, we came back to our dormitory.

In the evening, we came up to Mudumalai sanctuary and were astonished to see that the staff of T.N. wildlife department was waiting eagerly for our class to come. They had arranged everything for us. Actually Tamil Nadu people did not confirm our programme in writing, so we came direct to Bandipur. Mr. Nair felt sorry for not alighting there and now decided that our class comes to Mudumalai next morning and stay there also for one day at least. Mr. Nair called us in the night and instructed us to move to Mudumalai after breakfast, next morning. He himself was, first to go to the forest with Mr. John Singh to take photographs of Sambars at a waterhole and then to Mysore, to take some pugmark tracings of Zoo tigers. Later, he was to join us directly at Mudumalai on the next morning, on our way to Coimbatore. No body was to accompany Mr. Nair during the forest trip, except Mr. John Singh. We were not even asked to get up early and bid him goodbye, when he was to move into the forest in the early morning. Perhaps the destiny and his stars were manipulating the things in a very subtle way.

I still remember the morning 'coughs', the familiar coughs of Mr. Nair, that he was having that morning just out side our dormitory before leaving for the forests. Though I was awaken by that time, I remained in my bed, so also my other colleagues, as we were asked not to worry about him on that morning (the fateful morning). After some time, both of them were gone and we were waiting

Fig. 3.1: Late Mr. N.R. Nair, the Director (with Beard and Cap) with Trainees

for the bed tea to come. It was winter and was quite chilly out side. So we used to take tea in our sleeping bags only. After about half an hour or so (6.45 a.m.), we were taking our tea, when suddenly the big door of our dormitory opened with a bang and our taxi-drivers came dashing in, obviously terror stricken. They were shouting "your Director is no more, your Director died, killed by elephant". For a few moments we all were frozen. And then all of us rushed outside, in whatever attire we were, to know the facts. Outside we saw Mr. John Singh alone lying and rolling on the ground, in a 'shock'. He was crying and shivering and was almost hysterical. We all consoled him and taking him in confidence, asked him about the incidence. The following was his narration:—

Mr. Nair and Mr. John Singh were moving slowly, on foot towards the waterhole. It was still not very bright and little darkness persisted. At about one and a half kilometres away from Bandipur camp, when they were walking on the left side of the road (on 100′ clearance, created by the department on either side of the road for better visibility of the animals), they heard some branches of trees being broken by an elephant, a little ahead of them. John Singh stopped there to look out for the animal. After some efforts, they could locate a lone young tusker on the right side of the road beyond the clearance. It was hidden behind the trees. It had already taken the scent of Mr. Nair and Mr. John Singh as it lifted its trunk up and moved it in different directions, to discern the direction of human approach. Mr. John Singh was scared and asked Mr. Nair to change the route, so that they could avoid that tusker. The straight distance was around 150′, on a flat land with no hindrance or obstacle in between. But Mr. Nair insisted to stay back there only. Perhaps in the corner of his mind, he wanted to remove the fear of elephants from the mind of Mr. John Singh, and this was the best opportunity. After a few seconds, Mr. Nair decided to take a photograph of this very elephant. He moved 10-15′ further ahead to have a clear vision of the animal. Although Mr. John Singh tried to dissuade him from this venture, but being so junior (and a no body in the official capacity), he could not stop an officer of the forest department as senior as Mr. Nair was. He was looking desperately at Mr. Nair. Suddenly he saw that the tusker started running towards them. Now when an elephant is charging towards you from a distance of 150 feet and you are standing only 10 to 15′ apart, you can't say whom the elephant is charging at. Sensing danger, Mr. John Singh turned around and started running to save his own life. Mr. Nair, who could see the charging elephant through his camera, perhaps did not get much time to follow suite. On the contrary, he threw his camera towards the elephant to divert its attention and tried to climb up a small nearby Gmelina tree. He went little up, then slipped down due to the wet soles of his hunter shoes (the shoes got wet due to morning dew). Then Mr. Nair tried to rush into the Lantana bushes beyond the clearance behind him, but that is no hurdle for an elephant. When the elephant gave a trumpet call (a call generally of victory), Mr. John Singh turned around some distance away and tried to locate Mr. Nair. He called for Mr. Nair for a few times. There was no reply. The elephant had left the site after giving that 'victory call'. So, Mr. John Singh gathered some courage and came back to find Mr. Nair's still body under Lantana bushes. He called again and on getting no reply, rushed back to the camp. He informed at the reception counter and our taxi-drivers about the accident and who in turn brought the terrible news to us.

By that time, the forest staff had already kept one vehicle ready to go to the spot. We all got in to it with Mr. John Singh and came to the spot. We were shocked to find Mr. Nair's dead body, lying under the Lantana bushes. Police at Bandipur was informed, so also the Field Director, Project Tiger at Mysore. By 7.30 a.m. this sad news was given to P.R.I., Dehradun and the Principal Chief Conservator of Forest, Kerala State also. After due formalities, the dead body was removed from the spot and brought to Bandipur. The body apparently was not damaged much except that the blood was oozing out from skull and all orifices, i.e. nose, ear etc. The left upper arm was broken and the bone had come out of the skin. Since no body had seen the actual sequence of attack, we could only guess from the out come of the post-mortem conducted at Bandipur. Perhaps the elephant caught hold of left upper arm and lifted him with a jerk, which resulted in the broken arm, then rolled him in its trunk, breaking six of Mr. Nair's ribs. The elephants finally banged him on the ground, which caused the skull fracture. It did not trample the body under its feet otherwise the whole body would have been mutilated.

This was a tragic loss to our Directorate, Kerala State, to our country and a personal loss to his family and all of us. We can never forget him, his devotion to the wildlife and that fateful day. Yes! That was the only day when we were not with him. We had no words to answer the questions from Mrs. Nair. Since then I started believing in the horoscope and the stars. This gave us one lesson also that howsoever much experienced one might be, one must not put his life at risk with wild animals, they are all unpredictable. First we must arrange for our own safety, and then deal with such animals.

In this context I would narrate one more story. We were undergoing a training on 'immobilization of wild animals and radio-telemetry' at Corbett National Park. Dr. U.S. Seal and Dr. Mech had come from U.S. to impart this training programme. I was acting as a trainee-coordinator for around twenty trainee officers from all over India. After spending one week at Delhi Zoo, we had come to Corbett, mainly to tranquillize an elephant. At Dhikala, after two days wait, suddenly Dr. Seal came out of his room at 3.30 p.m. and gathered all of us also. He started preparing his equipment and side by side was asking whether any of us had experience with wild elephants. None of us had worked with wild elephants. Then I told him that we do not have wild elephants in M.P., but I had only one experience of wild elephants and that was the one in which Mr. Nair had lost his life. I narrated the incident. Dr. Seal had received information of one lone tusker which was seen on the bed of Ramganga river, about five kilometres away from our camp and he was preparing to tranquillize it. I told him that it would be very unsafe to attempt tranquillizing a lone tusker in an open area like the river bed of Ramganga and that he might be in no position to defend himself in case of a charge from that tusker. Paying due respect to my advice he immediately wound up the equipment and decided to wait further, for a better situation. Subsequently, we tranquillized a female from a herd next day, certainly without any danger or risk.

Episode-IV

The Survival of the Story-teller

During our wildlife training, we were in Kashmir. At Dachigam sanctuary, there was one enclosure of the Hangul deer, in which one single full grown female was kept. Actually the male partner had died a few days earlier. The enclosure was having about 10′ high chain-link fencing all around. As we were looking inside, the lone occupant, the female Hangul appeared at a little distance away from the fence. I was trying to take its photograph with my normal box camera. At that time, the Superintendent of the sanctuary came there and said "why are you taking the photograph from such a far distance, why don't you go in side and take a snap from a closer distance". I welcomed the suggestion. Climbed up the ladder and entered the enclosure. Mr. Sukhdev (now C.C.F., W.L., Tamil Nadu) was standing on the roof of Musk deer's enclosure and Mr. Khan from Andaman was standing and looking from out side the fence, rest of the class was busy in the lecture by Superintendent of the sanctuary.

As I was descending the ladder inside the enclosure, the deer came quite near. I may tell you that hangul is a huge deer. This one in particular was well fed and was of the size of a good big size cow. It approached the caretaker, who was standing near my ladder. He caressed her by patting and moving his hand under her neck. A very friendly gesture. As I got down, it came to me. I also moved my hand like the caretaker. It was perfectly O.K. She licked my hand and was quite friendly. Then I moved a little away, lifted my camera to take a snap. As I was focusing on her, she suddenly lifted her fore limbs high in air and charged at me. I may tell here that in the deer family the females do not possess antlers, so they defend themselves and even attack with the help of their hooves of forefeet. These hooves are razor sharp and can tear open one's skull if hit hard. I was shocked, so also was the caretaker. My batch mates Mr. Sukhdev and Mr. Khan too were awe struck watching helplessly from out side. It had never happened in our lives earlier. As her hooves came down, I moved a little backward and it brushed all along my length, from chest to toe. I could save my head but tumbled over some boulders behind me. I fell down, and then she lifted her limbs again for the second charge. But to my good luck, the caretaker had recovered from the first shock of his life by then. Immediately he lifted a twig from the ground and scared her off. I got up and rushed towards the ladder. She again came to me running, but by that time I was safely out of its reach. I took its photograph, then from the ladder. Then I came out the same way, as I had gone in. Both my colleagues also took a sigh of relief. But then I could never know the reason of its annoyance. Perhaps she did not like the camera being focused on her or was probably in a bad mood after losing her mate a few days earlier. I am still alive to narrate this incidence. But this also taught me a lesson that howsoever friendly these cute looking animals may be, they remain unpredictable and can harm us, any time. We must never take liberties with wild animals.

Episode-V

Three Days with the Tigress Khairi

We had heard a lot about 'Khairi' the tigress and were keen to see her. Luckily when I was posted in Kanha in 1978, I got an opportunity to meet Mr. Saroj Raj Chaudhary, the then Field Director, Simlipal Tiger Reserve, Orissa. It was First International Symposium on Tiger. Dr. P.C. Kotwal, Research Officer, Kanha, Mr. V.B. Sawarkar, Dy. Director, Melghat and Mr. R.C. Sahay, Dy. Director, Palamau Tiger Reserve and I were made the rapporteurs during the symposium. After the symposium was over, we were assigned the duty to prepare the minutes also. And during this process, we all assembled at Palamau and then at Simlipal. Mr. S.R. Chaudhary was returning to Khairi Jashipur, where 'Khairi' tigress was kept by him. We asked him if he could take us along with him in his jeep and show us his famous tigress. He gladly accepted to take us along with him. Director, Project Tiger, GOI, also gave us an official letter to go to Simlipal and complete the remaining work under the guidance of Mr. Chaudhary.

After lunch, we left Palamau at about 2.00 p.m. along with Mr. Chaudhary in his jeep. On way he told us all about this tigress 'Khairi', her age, size, habits, etc. We were really thrilled by the thought of seeing such a remarkable tigress.

At Khairi Jashipur, one Forest Rest House, that has four suites, was converted into the residence of Khairi. A small chunk of forest was also enclosed along with the main building by a chain link fence all around. We reached at Jashipur, at about 11.00 p.m. Mr. Chaudhary had already sent information on wireless about our arrival. At the entrance, we enquired about our queen Khairi's whereabouts at that moment and we were informed that she had gone to the forest patch. At the Rest House, on the right side of the dining hall were two suites which were permanently occupied by Khairi and her foster parents, i.e. Mr. Chaudhary and Ms. Nihar. This arrangement included the dining hall also. Two suites on the left side were meant for the visitors. So we were lodged in one of those suites. Mr. Chaudhary asked us to get fresh in ten minutes and come for dinner, which was ready. We hurriedly changed and joined him for the dinner. After dinner we were left in our room with the instructions to bolt the door from inside during night, because Khairi could come at any time of the night and open the door to get our introduction, which was really not needed till next morning.

We had a peaceful night. In the morning, Dr. Kotwal, being an early riser, got up and got ready also much early. By about 8.00 a.m., he opened the latch of the door and was sitting on his bed, just adjacent to the door. I was about to enter the bathroom, with towel wrapped around my waist. And then suddenly our door opened with a big bang. Lo! The queen of that empire was there, a huge fully grown tigress (about 10′ long). Khairi stood in the door, half in and half out, for a few seconds and gave out a restrained growl, as if enquiring about the new intruders. After that, she went towards Dr. Kotwal, who was sitting on his bed with his legs down. With a similar growl she rubbed whole of her body length with Dr. Kotwal's legs. Though we were told about her this particular behaviour of getting introduction of the new comers, nevertheless we were spell-bound at that moment. I was frozen at the door of the bathroom. When she was rubbing her body with Dr. Kotwal, he could muster some courage and murmurred 'Khairi, Khairi', praying her to spare him. I was looking on and waiting for my turn, which was inevitable. Yes! Then she came to me and rubbed her whole body with my legs and entered the bathroom in a mood to inspect it. She again came back in our room and climbed over the third spare bed, which was kept in front of the door of the bathroom. One can imagine this scene: a full grown tigress standing on a bed, reaching the height of your chest and continuously giving out subdued growls. There was no body with her, except we two strangers. We were cautiously observing her move and praying her not to misunderstand us. At that time, somebody had informed Mr. Chaudhary about her entry in our room. He immediately rushed to our room, calling his darling Khairi. He told her that we were guests and then took her along with him. We also told him about our introduction parade. Mr. Chaudhary said that now there was nothing to worry, she may or may not come to us at all. She has assured herself of these two new comers.

After breakfast, we had a round of the entire area, meeting other members of that great family, i.e. Jumbo (the Bear cub), Bhaina (a blind Hyena), Civets. etc. We were sitting with Mr. Chaudhary in his office room. He was busy with his files. Suddenly, something wriggled in his shirt, he caught hold of it and took out. It was a small crocodile; he kissed him and again put it into his shirt. After a while, there was a wriggling movement on other side of the shirt and this time it was a young mongoose, he kissed him too and put again into his shirt. He really loved animals and devoted his whole life to these small and big denizens of the wild. Then, as we came to the verandah, Khairi, who was sitting near fence, came rushing to me. She rubbed her body affectionately and sprayed her scent on my pant. Now I was her 'property'. She had strong liking for some persons. That whole day she remained near us only and played with us. We took a number of photographs also.

Fig. 5.1: Khairi, at her Residence Jashipur

Fig. 5.2: Author with Khairi

Fig. 5.3: Khairi on her Dining Table

Fig. 5.4: Khairi with author and Dr. Kotwal

Next day, we left for Chahala, an interior Forest Rest House in Simlipal Tiger Reserve and stayed there for two days. On the third day we came back to Jashipur. Once again Khairi came to me and was happy to meet us again. On the last morning, as we were taking our breakfast, she came to me and kept her head in my lap. She kept on sitting like that for whole of the time, till we ate our breakfast. One can imagine the feeling I was experiencing, when such a huge tigress kept her massive head in my lap, intermittently lifting her mouth towards mine, her breath coming full into my face. I cannot forget those extraordinary moments with that great tigress. She was really very affectionate, docile, 'gentle lady', lovable to all. I had that opportunity to live with her for three days, it was our good luck. It was an experience of life, which taught us many things. This hand reared tigress did not have the fear of man and had a strong liking for some people. She was so sure of human beings and therefore, never attacked anybody for self-defence. Although she had injured many forest guards on duty, even Mr. B.N. Naik, Deputy Director was badly injured, but the reason was different. During her last days she picked up 'Rabies' from perhaps a dog and bit Mr. Naik's arm. Subsequently she was made to sleep with high dose of tranquillizers.

Tigers are certainly gentler than the humans; unless we intend to harm or disturb them on a kill or while the mother is with cubs. We should not cross the limits, keep a safe distance, respect this graceful animal and enjoy its presence in nature.

Episode-VI

Elephant Purchased from Sonpur Fair

In wildlife wing of Forest Department, especially in National Parks, Elephants are purchased or acquired from other states. They are mainly used for Elephant safari in the wildlife parks. In M.P., they have been purchased or acquired departmentally from other states having wild elephant population or elephant rearing camps, such as Karnataka, Kerala, Tamil Nadu, etc. Our elephants are required. only to carry tourists for elephant ride or the 'Tiger show'. In olden days, a few were acquired for dragging timber in Bori Range of Hoshangabad Division. This practice of timber dragging has long been stopped in M.P. The Forest Officers in Madhya Pradesh do not come in contact with the elephants and its activities till they serve in one of such National Parks, which are maintaining elephants. Therefore, we are not aware of their behaviour also, as we are not having any wild elephant population in M.P. forests.

After Wildlife Management training at Dehradun, when I joined in Kanha National Park in 1978, I was not aware of the qualities of elephants required, and the procedure to purchase or acquire them. But certainly I enjoyed for a brief period of working with elephants in Bori Range of Hoshangabad Division during 1967-68. We had three elephants, namely Radha Pyari, Moti Pyari and Bataiyya Pyari. It was customary to feed the elephants daily ration of 9.00 kilos of wheat chapatties or rice laddoos, 1/2 kilo of jaggery (*gur*) in presence of the senior most forest officer, present that day in the camp. This ration used to be given in the evening time. Out of 9.00 kgs. Chapatties, one used to be saved to be given in the morning as breakfast. In the still older times, elephants were given pure ghee also, later on replaced by vanaspati and then omitted all together, perhaps due to pilferage and rising prices of these items. I don't know how far is it true that they used to feed 'chicken' also, some times in a month. This ration is not going to fill the large belly of an elephant, who needs at least 2.50 maunds of green fodder as daily diet. This ration feeding keeps a bond between 'mahaut' and the elephant, due to which the mahaut has a good control on the animal.

Well, in Kanha that year in 1978, our Chief Wildlife Warden had brought five elephants from Guwahati (one female Vandevi and four calves). One of the calves, i.e. Brahamputri had a broken scapula. It was presumed that either the people at Guwahati changed the calf while loading or may be it was injured during transit in the same truck in which all of these five elephants were transported from Guwahati. Anyhow this elephant in later years could not carry tourists on its back. It is still there in Kanha. All these years, she has been active in tracing the tigers. She has even given birth to two calves also so far; this has added two elephants in Kanha camp. After this experience at Guwahati, our Chief Wildlife Warden decided to purchase some more elephants from the Sonpur fair. The M.P. State Tourism Development Corporation agreed to finance this purchase. I was deputed to purchase four elephants from Sonpur. Now it was my duty to find out the dates of fair route to Sonpur from Mandla and other details. I never had earlier experience. The foremost thing required was, how to select good and the right animal. Our Head Mahaut, Mahabir was to accompany me to help me in this selection. But still I was very keen myself to know such qualities of a good elephant. From my friend Mr. S.M. Hasan, I could learn about one chapter in the book. The Highlands of Central India, written by great British officer, Capt. J. Forsyth, which had given good account of Sonpur fair and the quality of good elephants. It mentioned many things including good qualities of elephants. A few are mentioned below:

(1) Age of the animal: Younger the animal the longer the service you get from it. At that time, animals of shoulder height lower than four feet were not permitted to be caught or captured from the forests as they are very young and still feeding on mothers milk. An animal which can be straightaway harnessed with 'hauda' and can take tourists on its back, will certainly give longest service. The elephants with six feet shoulder height and above (15-20 years of age) are the best. On such animals the 'hauda' becomes about 10' high from the ground and one feels safe enough, near a tiger also. Age of the elephant can be judged from the folds of the skin on the upper margin of the ear pinna. Bigger the fold, the older it is. In older animals the 'pinna' of the ear also gets torn in many elephants. Even the inner side of the ears has got very tender and soft skin in young animals. Old animals do also have wrinkles and folds on the skin. More the number of wrinkles/folds, the older it is.

(2) Eye sight: Most of the animals coming to 'Sonpur mela' are having some eye defect or the other. As one of the elephant catchers (my friend Mr. Ramchandra Singh) told me, when you feed too much of Peepal leaves during summer months, these elephants develop cataract in their eyes and sometimes become blind also. So one has to check eyes carefully. You can move your fingers very close to the eyes on either side. If the elephant moves its eyelids, that shows no defect and that it can see normally. If the eyelids remain unmoved, one should know that the elephant cannot see. Such elephants are very dangerous for our works in the National Parks, especially in a tiger country.

(3) Kaandi: It is like a corn or canker in human beings. An animal with 'Kaandi' cannot walk for long distances. It pains and the animal will frequently stop for rest. Mahauts can see it on the sole of each foot. Sometimes the owners remove the superficial surface of the 'kaandi' with knife and fill sealing wax to make the sole smooth and flawless. It is done to cheat the purchasers. You can check the presence of 'kaandi' by tapping gently on the soles with help of blunt side of an axe, hammer or even stick. If elephant gives a jerk to its foot at a certain point, you can assume that it is having a 'kaandi' inside. You can reject such animals. Kaandi if not treated in time, will eat up deep in side the foot and break out above the toe nails.

(4) Split or broken nails: Some elephants have a tendency of having split nails now and then. Pus keeps on oozing from these nail wounds. Such animals also find difficulty in walking. One should reject such animals.

(5) Sajhan or the cracked heels: Like that of horse, deep cracks discharge matter and is situated between horny sole and the skin. It is also a serious defect and sometimes the animal is rendered useless during rains.

(6) Zeharbad: A condition generally which cannot be overlooked by a purchaser. It is of two types, *Asl* and *Sookha*. *Asl* zeharbad is caused due to sudden change in food of the animal, like feeding on only *Peepal* or *Bargad* leaves after capturing from the forest. It is a diseased condition due to swelling or oedema in which neck, chest and the stomach enlarge to an enormous size. The *Sookha* zeharbad developes out of the first or the *asl* one. It results in general atrophy or falling away which is characterised by shrivelled cracky skin much emaciation (becoming thin) and weakness. When much complicated, animal develops troublesome sores on various parts of the body. There should not be any doubt that such animals also need to be rejected.

(7) General shape of the animal: An elephant with a 'Kumra' or the Gourd like abdomen is called as 'Kumraband'. Such type of animals keep on eating whole day and are lazy workers. Most of the elephants have a little hump or arched backbone. When wooden 'hauda' is fitted on it, every now or then it gets hurt a wound or gall is formed, thereby rendering the animal off the job, for a few days for treatment. Therefore, the elephants with straight and flat back is the best for our National Parks. The 'hauda' fits very well on such backs. The slim looking animals are called 'Mrigaband' or 'deer like'.

(8) Rogue elephants: Some elephants are 'Rogue' by nature only. They are not faithful to their mahauts also. In Sonpur fair, even such elephants do come for sale. It is believed that owners of such elephants feed them with small dozes of Opium and Hemp during their stay in the mela, so that they remain docile before the prospecting purchasers. So one has to be very cautious regarding behaviour of such animals. An experienced mahaut can judge such behaviour immediately.

Fig. 6.1: Tonga Race at Sonpur Fair

The male elephants are temperamental and moody, therefore, it is better to purchase only females, if they are to be used for wildlife tourism.

Well, with no earlier experience, first I found the location of Sonpur on the map, then rail route via Allahabad and via Bhopal, Lucknow and Gorakhpur. Manager State Bank of India found out that there was no branch at Sonpur and the nearest one was at Hajipur. One of our mahauts in Kanha had sometimes gone to Sonpur and he guided us (rather misguided us) that the mela at Sonpur starts from the third day after Deepawali festival. So we decided to reach there accordingly. One forester, Ashok Shukla and Head Mahaut Mahabir Prasad were asked to go straight via Jabalpur, Allahabad, to Sonpur because I was to collect Bankdraft from Bhopal and reach there via Lucknow-Gorakhpur. That year Bihar had an epidemic of Encephalitis, a deadly disease. So at Lucknow, my relatives, asked me to postpone this trip or at least observe some precautions. Anyway I reached Sonpur at 12.30 p.m., both my forester and the mahaut met me at the station and informed me that there was no hotel or rest house of any type at Sonpur. So I continued my journey up to Hajipur. There they informed me that the mela was also to start only from the fifteenth day from Deepawali, i.e. on full moon day.

Now the first thing was to find a place to stay. Even at Hajipur, the P.W.D. dak bungalow was in a very bad shape. It was already occupied by some audit party. The irrigation Rest House was also not available. At Hajipur even so-called hotels were worse than any *Dharamshala* of Madhya Pradesh, only a '*takhat*' without bedding was provided, a common toilet, latrines overflowing with filth and nobody could tell me where to find the sweepers. In brief, no gentleman could stay in such a sham of a hotel. Now, where to go and what to do was the big question before me. I went back to the railway station and enquired about the retiring room. Yes! here I was lucky to get a bed in the newly constructed four bed dormitory. The other three beds were also vacant. It was really a good accommodation, but the allotment was only for two days. When I told my difficulty to the station master and said that I might be staying for fifteen days in all, as I had come to purchase elephants for Kanha National Park, he was kind enough to adjust me by renewing my allotment every second day, in one name or the other. The railway staff really helped me a lot and I thank them even today. Now was the question of getting safe food. I am a strict *chapati* eater and shun rice. At Hajipur that time no chapaties were available in most of the hotels. All were eating only *Chiwda* or *Poha* raw with curd water or anything. Actually, it was a district H.Q. of a newly constituted district 'Vaishali' and was yet underdeveloped. With great difficulty and efforts, one hotelier agreed to provide me with *chapaties*. And I obliged him by eating there for fifteen days. I deposited the bank draft in S.B.I. Hajipur and the then Manager, Mr. Baruah became a good friend of mine. All these days of waiting for the mela to begin, he used to come to me and take me around in his car and keep me entertained. Thanks to him for his hospitality.

But all this could not ward off fear of Encephalitis. Big posters were pasted on the walls on either side of the door of my retiring room, discouraging people from coming to the mela, due to encephalitis. I could not avoid reading the same warning every time I entered or came out of my room. When I came to Sonpur the next day, the mela site was being swept clean. The huge *maidan* of mela site had no sign of any animal. I talked with my Chief on phone and had no option than to stay back and wait for the mela to start.

About three days before the full moon day, i.e. '*Kartik Purnima*', the elephants started coming to the mela site, along with other animals such as buffaloes, cows, bull-ox, horses, etc. I saw almost each and every elephant that entered the mela (about 1000 elephants in all). It was really a sight to behold on the final day. Thousands of animals, all tethered to the pegs in well aligned rows. There were different sectors for different animals. Each animal having its own feeding place and nicely built drains, to lead the urine to the pits. The "*gobar*" or the dung was neatly collected immediately. All animals for sale were nicely decorated with different colours and ornaments of '*cowries*', the seashells. The biggest animal to be sold was elephant and the smallest being the Munia bird. In between you could name any animal (domesticated) and that was there. Camels, asses and even pups of different varieties of dogs were there for sale. It was really amazing. The elephant sector is very big along the banks of Gandak river and does not have any light or the electric poles, because elephants may uproot them. Otherwise the mela is very

Fig. 6.2: Elephant Race at Sonpur Fair

Fig. 6.3: Mr. and Mrs. Chaudhary, C.F. Wildlife, Waiting to take my Photograph

well lighted. Besides these animals, shops of different eateries, sweetmeat, utensils, clothes, cosmetics, sarees, shoes, furnitures, other households, etc. come to this mela. The main attraction of entertainment being '*Nautankies*', circus, '*Jhoolaghar*', etc. Everyday thousands of people come to this mela, some to purchase animals, others to enjoy.

I learnt that the main sale/purchase starts only after taking the holy dip in *Sangam*, the confluence of Ganges and the Gandak rivers on the full moon day. So though I saw all the good elephants in the mela but I was never disclosed the price till that holy day. One more special feature of the mela is that this large *maidan* of Sonpur is having a number of owners, each having a small chunk of land (or *khasras*). The owner of the animal comes from outside and tethers the animals on such small chunks (together forming a big *maidan*). As and when an animal is sold, a small cut/commission is charged by this owner of the land. It is known as *Kauri likhai*. Myself, my forester Shukla and mahaut Mahabir had come for the first time. Although we saw all the elephants, good and bad, males/females, but were not in a position to finalize the deal. I asked for quotations and was given a reply that no two elephants are alike, so no such quotations can be given; cost also varies from animal to animal. Generally, each trader brings 5-6 elephants to sell and has a small camp with a tent by the side of elephants, neatly tied in a row. On first day of sale, you can see all elephants, neat and clean after the morning bath, nicely decorated with ornamental clothes, cosmetics, garlands, etc. Each elephant could be seen with a *chara*-cutter sitting under its trunk near forefeet, feeding the elephant with small pieces of sugarcane wrapped in paddy. It is a beautiful sight—so many animals and men together, yet everything was absolutely clean. The local administration had used bleaching powder so liberally and they were really concerned about cleanliness, just to avoid any epidemic. Suddenly on one such camp, I came across one person, Mr. Ram Chandra Singh of Barabanki (U.P.), who had come to sell tall male elephants (five in number). They were really good animals. But we were interested in purchasing females only. Mr. Singh was an elephant catcher by profession. He was in the team engaged by U.P. Government. for catching elephants in Chila sanctuary in 1977. They used to catch small calves by '*mela shikar*' method. They caught 14 animals, out of which 7 died during capture. (We had seen those carcasses/skeletons during our visit to Chila, while under wildlife training.) I having come from forest department from M.P. Mr. Singh immediately became my good friend. He told me, "O.K. you may not purchase my elephants, come on I will tell you which animal to be purchased and which is not". He had been coming to these melas for many years and knew almost all others who were in this trade. He recognized all good and bad elephants, which were coming to this mela, year after year, with different owners. He showed me some very good looking elephants, who had killed their mahauts or other villagers in different places. He became my guide and we purchased three females and got co-operation from the owner to tether them there at one of such camp sites.

Now the arrangement was to be done for their transport to Kanha. That time in 1978, there was no bridge on Ganga river, hence, it was very difficult to get a truck on this side of the river. I had to go to Patna by a steamer. I needed three trucks to carry three elephants, and I was shocked to find that no truck owner/ driver were willing to give truck for elephants. The truck we needed was to have a National Permit, strong enough to bear the load of elephant and an expert driver, (the elephants are carried in standing position and as such sometimes on turnings, due to elephants load moving to one side, the entire truck is pulled to one side and sometimes are over turned also.) No transporter was ready; I spent two days at Patna, searching for trucks. Secondly, I was worried about my elephants, which I had purchased. Actually all elephants look alike and I was afraid that if somebody stole my elephants in the night, how to and where to search for it. We would not be able to tell the police any identification mark also. One thing I had done immediately after purchase was that I wrote with white paint in big letters on the sides and ears of each elephant "Kanha National Park". That was the only identification we had.

I went to T.C.I. (Transport Corporation of India), Patna and The State Transport Corporation, both said no. Actually about four years back somebody had taken four trucks to Sonpur to transport elephants, but none of the elephants could be loaded on these trucks and they were returned to Patna after three days without any payment. Since then the management had issued strict order not to carry elephants. I was really in a fix. I was quite desperate and gloomy when one more gentleman appeared on the scene—Mr. Singh, the manager of the Auto Transport Company. He became my saviour. He rang up to various agents and by the third day morning I got one truck. At about three in the afternoon, I got the second truck. Now they were ready to move to Sonpur, but without third truck how could I leave. One cannot imagine how upset I was. But Mr. Singh was very co-operative, who used to say, "why are you so upset, whatever delay has to take place, it will. We are trying our level best, what else can we do". Yes! he was correct. Then he said, let us send these two trucks to the ferry site from where they were to cross Ganga river by steamer. There also they had to stand in queue. So we sent them immediately. Luckily, the third and the last truck was also arranged at 6.30 p.m. and I rushed with this truck to the ferry site, about 25 kilometres away from city.

Oh God! here I found that even those two trucks were still standing in a long queue. Only two steamers were ferrying trucks from either banks of Ganga and about two hours were spent in each trip. One Bacha Babu was the owner of this steamer company. I tried to contact the manager saying that my elephants were Government purchase and if he could oblige us by sending us in the next trip (out of turn). No, he said. I was also informed that the last trip would be over by 10.30 p.m. After that one has to wait till the next morning. They could not ply the steamer in the night due to darkness and fog over the river. Somehow he agreed to oblige me in the last trip of the day, but then I was not that lucky. Later I came to know that the steamer which was to return to this bank after unloading was stuck up on the other bank itself. While unloading a truck which was carrying coal, its axle was broken and the truck half on land and half on the ramp had pegged the steamer to the bank. This entire coal was to be unloaded in the next morning, manually. The other steamer also could not go to that bank that night. Now I was asked to come the next morning. The big question for me was that would these trucks wait for me, already they had wasted one day. Two trucks belonged to one Sardarji from Surguja M.P. and the owner was there with the trucks, a nice gentleman, he agreed to stay back till morning. The third truck driver was also somehow succumbed to my request and agreed to co-operate. But I decided to wait at the ferry site only. Going back to city was out of question. Once they agreed I started searching a place for me. Imagine, the icy month of December, a foggy night on the banks of Ganges and my poor self without any bed or baggage. The steamer company was having only a few benches for waiting passengers. No food was available. I tried to stretch myself on one of the benches, but I was frozen in half an hour. Cool breeze coming from Ganges was just biting into my bones. Then, suddenly I found that Sardarji appeared on the scene as an 'angel' for me, he had come with a new blanket and said, "how can you spend the whole night like this, we don't have enough room in the truck cabin but we can spare this blanket for you". I thanked that gentleman and somehow spent that night with the help of this blanket. Had it not been there, certainly I would have died with pneumonia on the bank of Ganges on that night.

Next morning, we were permitted in the first trip which started at about 10.30 a.m. There on the steamer were eight trucks in all. After some time, I found one lean and thin, beggar like person coming to me. He hesitated a bit and then asked in English, if I could understand English. I said, "yes" He was overwhelmed with joy. He was a 'Keralite' who didn't know Hindi, and had come to Sonpur to purchase elephants about one and a half month back. He kept on searching for elephants in the villages around, but was very upset as none knew English and he did not know Hindi. These past months he could not eat properly as he could not get South Indian (Keralite) food. I could not stop laughing, when he showed me his wrist and said, "see, how weak I have become, my mother will cry when I go back". Anyhow, he had purchased five elephants and was carrying five trucks for their transportation. I had seen him two days earlier in T.C.I.'s office also.

We reached Sonpur with our trucks. His trucks were loaded on steamer after my trucks, so were unloaded first. Therefore, his trucks reached the mela site earlier than ours and occupied the elephant loading ramps first. My elephants and the staff were safe and we also started preparing for loading our elephants. The elephants were put '*bedies*', i.e. iron-cuffs on forefeet, ropes are also tied with a noose on the neck and then the experienced mahaut sits on elephant back with

'*Ankush*' (a pointed iron weapon to control the elephant). The helpers with long spears, slowly move the elephant on ramp first and then on to the truck. It is very slow and cautious move. Once an elephant develops some doubt about the truck, it might take hours to convince it and to load. A suspicious elephant might jump from the ramp, truck and starts running like a 'rogue'. My Keralite friend loaded two elephants in one hour, but the third one started to misbehave. It began jumping and was not willing to go up into the truck. This belligerent behaviour was beginning to disturb my docile elephants also. After two hours of futile efforts, I got wild and asked this friend of mine to remove his elephants from the ramps, get them sedated by some veterinary doctor and come again after I have loaded my elephants. I threatened him to break his 'thin' wrists if he did not do that. It worked and I loaded my elephants by 9.30 in the night and the trucks were moved on their journey to Kanha National Park.

Next day, I caught a train to Lucknow and then way back to Mandla. I was relieved to find that my elephants had reached safely at Kanha. These elephants were the best of the whole lot, a number of customers came to purchase these from us, while they were standing at the mela site. At the time of loading one Mr. Baruah from Guwahati, came to me and congratulated me on this purchase, these being the best elephants. Incidentally, it was he who got the elephant 'Vandevi' purchased by Mr. J.J. Dutta, our C.W.L.W. from Guwahati, a few months back.

This was my first purchase, but was very satisfying. But then fear of 'Encephalitis', difficult conditions at Hajipur, Sonpur, etc. made me lose five kilograms of weight in fifteen days time. Moving in mela along with lacs of rupees in cash was quite risky. Even taking police help was more risky in Bihar. I was safely back and that was great.

During this trip I learnt a few more things about elephant fairs, where elephants were sold in Bihar and Uttar Pradesh, and other general things which are:—

(1) Khagra mela: Takes place during the month of '*Poos*', at the time of '*Khichari*' (*Makar Sankaranti* – winter equinox), i.e. from 14th January. One could reach the nearest railway station of Kishanganj by train. The mela used to run for two and a half months to three months and all new elephants used to be sold in this mela.

(2) Sitamarhi mela: Starts mid of *Agahan,* i.e. last week of November. A mela of only one week duration. One had to reach through Muzzafarpur. It was better to reach the mela site by *dwitya,* i.e. 22nd or 23rd November.

(3) Singeshwarsthan mela: One could reach Mansi junction by A.T. mail. From there to Madepura via Saharsa. The site is about three kilometres from Madepura. It started from *Shivratri* in *Phagun* month, i.e. March. It was advisable to reach 2-3 days in advance of *Shivratri*.

(4) Tadhwamath mela: At Tadhawamath in Betia, it is located in West Champaran district of Bihar. It used to start five days before Deepawali to '*Chhath*'.

It was new mela only two years old started in 1978. Very small number of elephants used to come for sale.

(5) Village Saidpur, district Badaun (U.P.): It used to start from middle of *Poos* on *'amawas'* day, i.e. during December month. It is located on Badaun-Chandausi road, easily approachable by road, buses and taxies are available.

One should note that these fairs were being held in 1978. At that time elephant capture was permitted in many Eastern States, from where these elephants were being brought to these fairs. As these days elephant capture from the wild is prohibited, I am not sure whether these fairs are still held or not. In case some body wants to visit such melas, he must confirm the details preferably from Forest Department or any other suitable source.

There at Sonpur mela, some Government land is reserved for various departments. Small plots are allotted by the Collector Chhapra District of Bihar, where one could erect his tented camp during the period of Sonpur fair. I got such allotment during my second trip in 1979, fifteen days in advance. Now at least Forest Officers (even from other states) do not require such arrangement, because Forest Department of Bihar State establishes such camp at Sonpur. D.F.O., Saran Extension Division, Chhapra remains present through out the fair period. Forest Officers who come to mela, can stay in this camp. It is advisable to contact and inform D.F.O., Chhapra in advance.

During my second trip in 1979 the conditions were made easy by our C.W.L.W. He had then permitted me to take a jeep and sufficient staff including a Forest Ranger, a Forester, two mahauts, a Baira and a Cook. Although, I got a plot booked for setting up my camp at the mela, we were lucky to get one house on the out skirts of mela on rent, where we could all stay together and keep our elephants also. This time also I purchased three elephants. One of these elephants this time troubled us in loading. After reaching inside the truck, it used to turn around and face backwards and get down. We enticed it with sweets (the Ranger brought only one kg. of *laddoos*), she came up and finished in one swing only and again turned around and half way on the ramp. Then I went to the market and brought five kgs. of *laddoos* in a big plate (*Paraat*). Again for sweets she came up to eat, the body of the truck was closed immediately, preventing her to get down again. It was night time and as all the lanterns and Petromax were on backside, she started again moving around before it could be fixed inside. I tried to pull its ears and keep her straight but all in vain. Ultimately, we had to fix her facing backwards only and sent her in this position to Kanha. It is a dangerous position, because the elephant can jump on the open side. But we had no choice. Luckily, these also reached quite safely.

Third time, I was posted as Director, Madhav National Park, Shivpuri. One day I got a phone call from the then C.W.L.W., that I had to go to purchase elephants. I objected and requested him to send some officer from Kanha or other park, where the elephants are needed. He said, "No! only you have to go as no other officer knows how to purchase elephants from Sonpur. Ultimately I conceded with a condition that some other officer may also be sent with me to learn the procedure. And this time, Mr. H.S. Pabla, the then Director, Panna National Park was asked to accompany me to Sonpur. We both started from Shivpuri by jeep to go via Lucknow, Gorakhpur, Chhapra. On way I was telling him all the stories of my previous purchases and we reached Chhapra at about 5.00 p.m. Mr. Pabla was inclined to stay there for the night, because going further 40-45 kms. and then searching for a place to stay would have been a torture again. I told him that the mela had already started three days back, we were very late, and so it would be better to reach Sonpur in the night itself. Suddenly we could see a board with D.F.O., Saran Division written on it (till '79, there was not even a forest guard on this side of river Ganges). When we enquired there about the D.F.O., we were informed that the D.F.O. was in the camp at Sonpur and we could also stay in that camp. What a great relief we thought and immediately rushed to Sonpur. We were warmly welcomed by the D.F.O., who was alone in the eight tented accommodation. It was a very well established camp with electricity, water and attached lat-bath, what more could one want. Even a mess and a lounge were also there. They accommodated our support staff also. We were satiated with this unexpected hospitality extended to us. We thanked our luck and the generous D.F.O.

The next morning, we began scouting for suitable elephants very early. Many good elephants were already sold. Somehow, we got two females and for the first time had to go for one male. There was no option. Then, we had no idea that a team of photographers was investigating our whereabouts. That evening, we were being searched by a party of photographers to shoot us. None other than, the great family of Bedi films (all three, Ramesh, Naresh and Rajesh). They got information at Delhi that I was at Sonpur to purchase elephants and as they had a project in their hands "*Ganesha*, the elephant god," they immediately rushed to Patna by air and then to the fair to search for us. Altogether a new experience this time. We were asked to enact the scene of elephant purchase again and the film was made.

By this year, the longest bridge on Ganges linking Patna city with Hajipur had come up, facilitating hassle free movement across the river. We came to Patna and could book the trucks easily and paid advance also. Till now Mr. Pabla was very happy, so was I, as we had faced no hindrance or difficulty. Next day we waited whole day for our trucks with Bedi brothers, but the trucks did not turn up. We came back to Patna changed the agency and booked the trucks elsewhere. The trucks, as usual reached Sonpur next evening at about 5.00 p.m. We were ready to load our elephants, so immediately started our work. This time Mr. Pabla went and contacted a senior local mahaut of about 75 years age, to load our elephants. Well, our male elephant Mohan Bahadur and one female took no time to be loaded. By about 8.00 p.m., they were up on their trucks. Now our third one to be loaded was a real hard nut to crack. It was already two hours past and our mahaut was still struggling. Another one hour later, our elephant was climbing up the ramp in reverse direction. Half way, it got stuck up. In the meantime, Mr. Pabla asked for a short leave and went back to the camp. This was the time when our male elephant had broken the top wooden bars of the truck on which it was loaded. Then we also discovered to our dismay that it had made a hole in the cabin with its tusk. The truck driver was panicky and angry. I calmed him down and told him to have patience. I tried to explain to him that when huge elephants are loaded on to fragile wooden truck bodies, such mishaps are normally expected. I gathered all my mahauts and made them to control the disobedient elephant. During this trip one more new thing had happened. Ansari, the forest ranger was from my park—Madhav National Park, Shivpuri who had never seen an elephant earlier. The head Mahaut, Mahabir was from Kanha and the other mahaut Nair was from Bandhavgarh, both had their own weird way of thinking and I had a suspicion that they disliked each other. This strange combination of my team members created a lot of confusion at the time of loading the elephants on to the trucks.

At about mid-night, our lanterns were very dim due to soot of carbon, the old mahaut once again tried to push the elephant up with the help of spears, tears were coming out from the eyes of the elephant and then one of the spectators shouted "*aye mahaut, kya karte ho, dekhate nahin, haathi ro raha hai, kyon bhala chubhate ho*" (Aye mahaut can't you see that the elephant is weeping, why are you poking it with the spear). On hearing this, our old mahaut got wild and shouted back to him "*mujhko haathi load karna sikhate ho, main hazaron haathi truckon par charha chuka hoon*" (you are teaching me how to load elephants on to the truck, I have loaded thousands of elephants on the trucks) and with this he left the scene and vanished in the darkness of the night. I did not know his camp or the resting place. So I was looking at my elephant halfway up on the ramp and sat on a cot to wait for some time. When, Mr. Pabla came back, he was told all about it. As he left again to bring mahaut back to work, several mahauts started shouting in the dark at him "*kaun hai udhar haathi ke paas, marna hai kya, haathi do log ko maar chuka hai*" (Who is there near that elephant, do you want to die, it has killed two persons already). And they surrounded him. Then he clarified and told them that he was going to call our old man back. He told them that the elephant had spared him then why did they want to kill him. Anyhow, he searched the old man and brought him back on the unfinished job. Now with new zeal and power we again engaged ourselves, because our other elephants were getting restless now. Our third elephant now jumped from the ramp and broke it also (earthen ramp). We shifted to another more sturdy ramp. Time was over 2,00 a.m., by then most of the helpers and spectators had vanished. As the elephant started moving up the ramp, two ropes tied with the neck noose had to be pulled through wooden railing of the truck body, one on either side. Pabla offered to pull one side rope. At one point, I found our old mahaut shouting at Mr. Pabla, saying "*aye sardar, munh kya dekhta hai, rassa kyon nahin kheenchata*" (aye sardar, why are you looking at my face, why don't you pull the rope). He never knew that this was our one of the senior officers and not just a sardar. I could not stop my burst of laughs along with Mr. Pabla and then he sincerely started pulling the rope. This way we could complete loading the elephant only around 4.00 a.m. We came back to our tent and dropped dead after an almost twelve hours, non-stop exercise. The trucks were gone.

After two hours, when Mr. Pabla was still fast asleep, my Ranger Ansari appeared, quite panicky, saying "sir, the elephant has broken all his chains and ropes and is jumping in the truck near Hajipur. I want to purchase more chains and ropes and want to take that mahaut with me to Hajipur I gave him my jeep and permitted him to carry all that he wanted to. He didn't want me to accompany and assured that he would manage the situation, so I stayed back. At 9.00 a. m. Pabla woke up, evidently from a deep and much needed sleep. He was happy and said at last they have moved. Then I told him about the morning frantic call of my Ranger. We thought, by now they must have 're-fixed' the elephants and moved on as there was no further call for help. Pabla said," let us go to Hajipur, close our account in the bank, have a hearty meal in some good hotel (we were very hungry, as we did not have our dinner last evening). Thereafter, Mr. Pabla wanted to leave by train for Allahabad, on way to Panna. We came to Hajipur, till then our jeep had not come back. At about 12.30 p.m., as we were standing on road out side the hotel after lunch, we saw our jeep coming from the side of Patna town. From a distance, I could see only Puran, my driver in it. We were relieved. As Puran got down from jeep, I asked him if everything was fine and then he quietly handed over a letter from Ranger Ansari. It said, "*sir, haathi ne phir rassa tod liya hai, control nahin ho raha hai, mahaut log bhi meri nahin sun rahe hai, mere dimag ne kaam karna band kar diya hai, kripaya aayiye aur mujhe bachayen*" (sir the elephant has broken the rope again and is not being controlled by mahauts, mahauts are not listening me any more, my brain has stopped working, please come and save me). Mr. Pabla was looking at my face. Then Puran said that by the time he turned his jeep, the trucks had started moving on their way to Kanha. So presuming everything alright, we started packing up ourselves.

At Patna station, Mr. Pabla was informed that only one train was there for Allahabad and that too Janata Express. He said, "No, I will go by first class only, may be from Sonpur itself". Again we came back to Sonpur, at the station after a lot of searching we found the first class counter—a small dilapidated window and a haggard clerk behind it. Mr. Pabla peeped inside and the clerk asked "*first class mein jayiyega?*" (will you go in first class?) Yes! said Mr. Pabla. Then the clerk turned his face and started smoking bidi. Pabla was annoyed and again asked him to give a ticket. Again was the question "*first class mein hi jayiyega?*". Now was the limit, Mr. Pabla asked him as to why was he asking the same question again and again, the reply was "*Saheb, first class to Gorakhpur tak jaate jaate lut jati hai*" (Sir, first class compartment is looted by the time it reaches Gorakhpur). Mr. Pabla was shocked but adamant to go by train. Then he changed his mind and purchased a ticket for second class sleeper. He sat in the train with his luggage on the upper berth. Suddenly a T.T. came and started asking whose luggage was that. Mr. Pabla said it was his. Then T.T. scolded him "can't you keep your luggage on the inner side, somebody will take it away and you will be complaining and blaming. Pabla was fully exhausted and prayed him "will you please let me go or not". Well there ended his training and our trip. I returned to Shivpuri by road. Fortunately, these elephants also reached Kanha safe and unhurt.

The last trip was in 1984, once again from Kanha I was busy at Jabalpur, trying to capture one leopard at C.O.D. There only came a call from Bhopal. C.C.F. (Wildlife) telling me to move to Sonpur to purchase elephants. So funny, the mela had already started, I said, "I am already away from my H.Q. for the last seven days, how could I go like this. It requires at least ten days preparing for this trip" But there was no excuse, because no one else knew 'how to purchase elephants from Sonpur'. Then I told him about Mr. Pabla who was trained all about this in the previous year. He said, "O.K., you come prepared to Bhopal, I will call Mr. Pabla also". Then from Bhopal one of you will go. Hurriedly, I gathered my staff from Kanha and reached Bhopal, only to know that Mr. Pabla was on holiday availing L.T.C., so I only had to complete the job.

I raced towards Sonpur and covered 850 km in one day up to Lucknow. Next day via Gorakhpur I rushed straight to the forest camp at Sonpur. This time there was another problem. When I reached there, I found D.F.O., Chhapra holding his head in his hands. This old man retiring in next six months time had a big problem at his hands. The Assistant Director (Wildlife Preservation, East Zone, Government of India) had arrived at the mela a day earlier to find out whether all provisions of *Wildlife Preservation Act*, 1978 were being followed strictly or not. And on finding that most of the elephant owners did not have ownership certificates from their respective C.W.L.W., asked D.F.O. to seize all such elephants and report. It had never happened in the history of Sonpur fair. That year, about 173 elephants had come for sale. If the D.F.O. had to seize even 150 elephants, how would he do it? The Asstt. Director could not bear the cold at the forest camp, so he had shifted to some hotel at Patna and was enquiring every one hour on telephone, whether the D.F.O. had seized the elephants. The D.F.O. had met the D.M. and the S.P., who in turn told him to do it at his own risk, and if any law and order problem arose, the D.F.O. would be responsible. Therefore the poor chap was holding his head totally confused. I told him the way out. For seizing 150 elephants, he would need 150 mahauts and the same number of *chara*-cutters with immediate effect. Whether so many people were available at Sonpur? For their daily wage and feeding the elephants on site at the rate Rs. 200/- per elephant per day, a huge sum would be required, whether he had that much fund available with him? So better write to your C.C.F. for allotment of fund (calculating for one week at least). If and when you get the funds and the people, you may start seizing the elephants otherwise not. I advised him to send a letter accordingly and inform the Assistant Director also. He did it and the very next day, their C.F. (Wildlife) Mr. Chaudhary also reached our camp for discussion on this problem. I was also included in the discussion along with D.M. and S.P. The Assistant Director was mainly concerned about the elephants which had come from Nepal. Others from U.P. and Bihar had either applied for ownership or were ready to apply now. So the Nepal elephants were asked to leave the mela and others who had applied were given certificates on the spot. This way the problem was solved.

This time I could purchase only two elephants. My elephants had come first and second in the elephant race conducted every year by the veterinary department of Bihar. I was informed that the prizes will be given away by the Governor of Bihar. Mr. and Mrs. Chaudhary were very happy and said that they will take my photographs while receiving the awards from the Governor. So we reached the function well in time. After races of all animals, like horses, *tongas*, bull-ox, etc. the inaugural speech was started by Director, Veterinary Department. It was very long and boring. The Governor was also bored and tired like us. So when he was invited to distribute the prizes, he gave away the prizes for best Buffaloes first and then said, "I am tired" and left for Patna. Now we were very sad and worried about my own prizes. So I sent my Ranger to ask the Director and was astonished to see the Director rushing towards me from amongst the crowd. He came to me, dragged me to the dais and introducing me announced on the mike that all the remaining prizes will be distributed by Mr. R.C. Sharma. It was another strange experience for me. Ultimately my prizes were given by the Director himself. There was no problem in transportation this time and all– men and animals reached safely.

That evening came the D.F.O. of Hazaribag, a friendly gentleman; he asked me whether I had an opportunity to watch a '*Nautanki*' in the mela. When I said no, he was astonished that even after coming to mela four times, I had never seen a *Nautanki*. Immediately he called for three V.I.P. tickets for "Bimla Nautanki" and we were there for almost the entire night and I came back only at 3.00 a.m. because I had to travel by road next morning on a long and tedious return journey. The *nautanki* was really an experience to remember.

This is the complete saga how I purchased eleven elephants from the Sonpur fair, for the Government of M.P. Most of these, later on multiplied at their respective camps and have added a good number of useful offsprings to our National Parks. I still remember the warnings of two of our officers, during the first purchase itself. Firstly, Mr. S.M. Hasan, told me that while he was going to Guwahati to help Mr. J.J. Dutta in purchasing elephants from there, his entire cash was stolen between Mughal Sarai and Howrah. He just took the next train available to Jabalpur, with just Rs. 150/-, which incidentally was left in his '*kurta*' pocket. Mr. Mamgain, another officer one day came to our office from Bilaspur and started asking as to who had purchased elephants from Sonpur. I said, 'I purchased'. Are they alright, was the next question. I said "yes, they are" and also asked him, why he was asking such questions. He said, "I purchased only one elephant from Sonpur for the Government of Bhutan, when I was on deputation and that too became a 'rogue' on the day Maharaja of Bhutan sat on it. The mahaut jumped from it when he could not control it and the Maharaja saved himself by holding on to some tree branch above him. I was about to lose my job because of it". Well god helped me and nothing of that sort happened with me.

As an *epilogue* to this tale, I would like to give some suggestions to all those who wish to purchase elephants even now from Sonpur, they must plan it, well in advance. The officer going for this job must be given at least 15 days time to prepare. He and his staff will have to make arrangements for ten to fifteen days for their family needs. Secondly, all the best elephants are sold in the first two days, because no one can afford to feed elephants for a longer time. The sellers and the purchasers both act very quickly as regards elephants disposal. So one must reach the site, two days before the mela starts, i.e. "*Kaartik Poornima*".

Episode-VII

The Child Lifting Wolves of Barhi

On 18th May, 1986, I was sitting at the table of D.F.O., Jabalpur Division, a message came from Barhi (near Katni) that a child was lifted and killed by some animal in Village Kuthia Mehgawan near Barhi. The D.F.O. said to me "Another assignment has come for you". That time, I was posted in Kanha Tiger Reserve as Deputy Director and was busy at Jabalpur planning the capture of a leopard, which was frequenting the ammunition factory area. I said, "OK, ask my Field Director for my services and I will be there." Kuthia Mehgawan is at about a distance of six kilometres from Barhi in South-West direction. The child was lifted in the day time, around 11.00 a.m. in an open field, adjacent to the forest. Subsequently, three more incidents took place within eight kilometre radius up to 18-6-1986. These were committed during nights and the children were lifted from their houses. The age of the victims, ranged from two months to four years, i.e. weightwise they were between 2 kg. to 15 kg. approximately. In all these cases, no part of the dead body was recovered during the search. But no one sought my assistance when all this was happening.

Then there was a sudden lull for about eleven months, when no incident took place from 19-6-1986 to 12-5-1987. Again from 13-5-1987 to 05-12-1987, twelve more cases of child lifting were reported. On 5-12-87 the child was lifted from an open field at 4.00. p.m. in Hatheda village. After this incident again there was a gap of about four months, when on 27-3-88, another child was lifted in Mohni village at mid-night.

Now the area of operation of this marauding animal extended over a radius of 17 kms. All these cases, except the one on 5-12-87, took place during night time. The children were mostly lifted from the houses located on the periphery of the villages. Now about two years had passed, children were being lifted and Director, Bandhavgarh National Park's services were being taken to identify and eliminate the animal. Then in 1988, when I was working as D.F.O., Social Forestry Division, Jabalpur, on 6th April I got a message from the Chief Wildlife Warden to proceed immediately to Barhi and join the mission to eliminate the animal which by that time had killed 18 children. Permission from C.C.F., Social Forestry was already granted. I talked with D.F.O., Jabalpur (incidentally my batch-mate, Mr. K.K. Parashar) and we agreed to start the next day in the after noon.

The next day, on 7-4-88 we started in the afternoon and reached a place called Jhiriya. Here in the nursery campus, a camp was already established in the forest rest house with wireless facility. The D.F.O. till then had mapped the entire operational area of the animal into three zones, i.e. Hatheda, Kuthia Mehgawan and Baragaon. Three well equipped patrolling parties were also formed as follows:—

1. H.Q. at Khitauli
    1. Mr. U. Khan, A.O.
    2. Mr. D. Singh, R.A. Khitauli
    3. Mr. Mishri Lal, F.G.
    4. S.A. F. Jawans—two
2. H.Q. at Jhiriya.
    1. Dr. P.C. Kotwal, Res. Officer, Kanha
    2. Mr. H.C. Sharma, Dy. R.
    3. Mr. M.Y. Khan, Fr.
    4. Mr. H.L. Sharma, Dy. R.
    5. F.G. Jawans—one.
    6. S.A.F. Jawans—one.
3. H.Q. at Barhi
    1. Mr. G.P. Dwivedi. S.D.O.
    2. Mr. J.N. Tiwari, Fr.
    3. Mr. Munir Khan, F.G.
    4. S.A.F. Jawans—two.

All these parties were provided with jeeps, binoculars, search lights, guns, wireless sets, etc. Barhi Range Office was the Control Station. The parties were instructed to patrol their respective zones, from 6.00 p.m. to 8.30 p.m. and then 10.30 p.m. to 4.00 a.m. in order to locate and eliminate the animal. Apart from above, informers in the shape of *chaukidars* were posted in seven different villages of various zones, who were supposed to inform any new development to the control room immediately. Trap cages were also installed in sensitive areas and even gin traps were kept ready to be planted whenever needed on the fresh tracks of the animal.

Compensation had been paid to the kin of the victims in all the previous cases. People in the area were cautioned to take necessary preventive measures, through local announcements and distributing pamphlets. A team of experts from Kanha and other adjoining parks were already camping in the field to accomplish the job. In addition, ten permits were issued to the local hunters for shooting the animal with a reward of Rs. 2000/-.

Before starting with my idea and planning, I preferred to watch for a day, as to what exactly were they doing in the field till now. The planning of the D.F.O. appeared to be perfect, apparently. Till dinner, I went through the map of the affected area and all the records of events happened so far. Then at 10.00 p.m., Parashar asked his driver to bring his open jeep. He was also equipped with one five cell torch and a twelve bore gun. We sat in the back seats along with one or two more staff members. He asked the driver to start the jeep and move towards Grauan village, about five kms. from Jhiria. A kill was made in this village on 21-3-88. This was a season of mahua collection and all around, people were occupying the ground under every mahua tree even during night. Some were living with lanterns, some had lit small fire to keep vigil. Even cattle were spread all over. We were driving in the night around these villages in the hope that the culprit animal will be seen somewhere and we will shoot it. Nothing was seen. Funniest thing was that till then they were not knowing the exact species of the culprit animal also. They had collected some hair from some spot and were trying to identify the animal with its help. So far they had been taking some help from the Director, Bandhavgarh National Park. In a field near a village, Parashar saw two eyes shining in the torch light; he got excited and urged me to shoot at that animal. I asked him whether he could identify that animal, he was not sure because only the eyes were visible. Then, I warned him not to shoot at any animal, aimlessly. I reprimanded him—"You are yet not sure as to which animal is killing these children, secondly, you cannot see in this torch light a complete animal in the night, this way you might shoot some domestic animal instead of the real culprit, thirdly, you might even accidentally hit a man out of these so many people sitting under these mahua trees, and if you do that, you will surely invite another major problem for yourself." Then he packed his gun and decided not to venture again in the dark. We came back after taking a round at about mid-night.

Next day, I discussed the possible next steps with the D.F.O. and then took a tour of Kua, Nadawan, Mohni and Bagaia villages. These villages lay basically in a plain area, yet strewn with a number of perennial nalas. No animal was seen. While returning, at Bagaia it was reported that while a woman had gone to return nature's call with her child in the evening on 7-4-88, she saw an animal approaching her child. She was alert and raised an alarm, as people ran to the spot, the animal fled. We met this brave woman and asked her about the animal' shape, size, etc. She said that it was quite dark and she could not see it clearly, but it was of the size of a dog and walked like a dog only. She pointed out a nearby nala which the animal had last used to escape from villagers. It became night, so we decided to come in the morning again to check the nala.

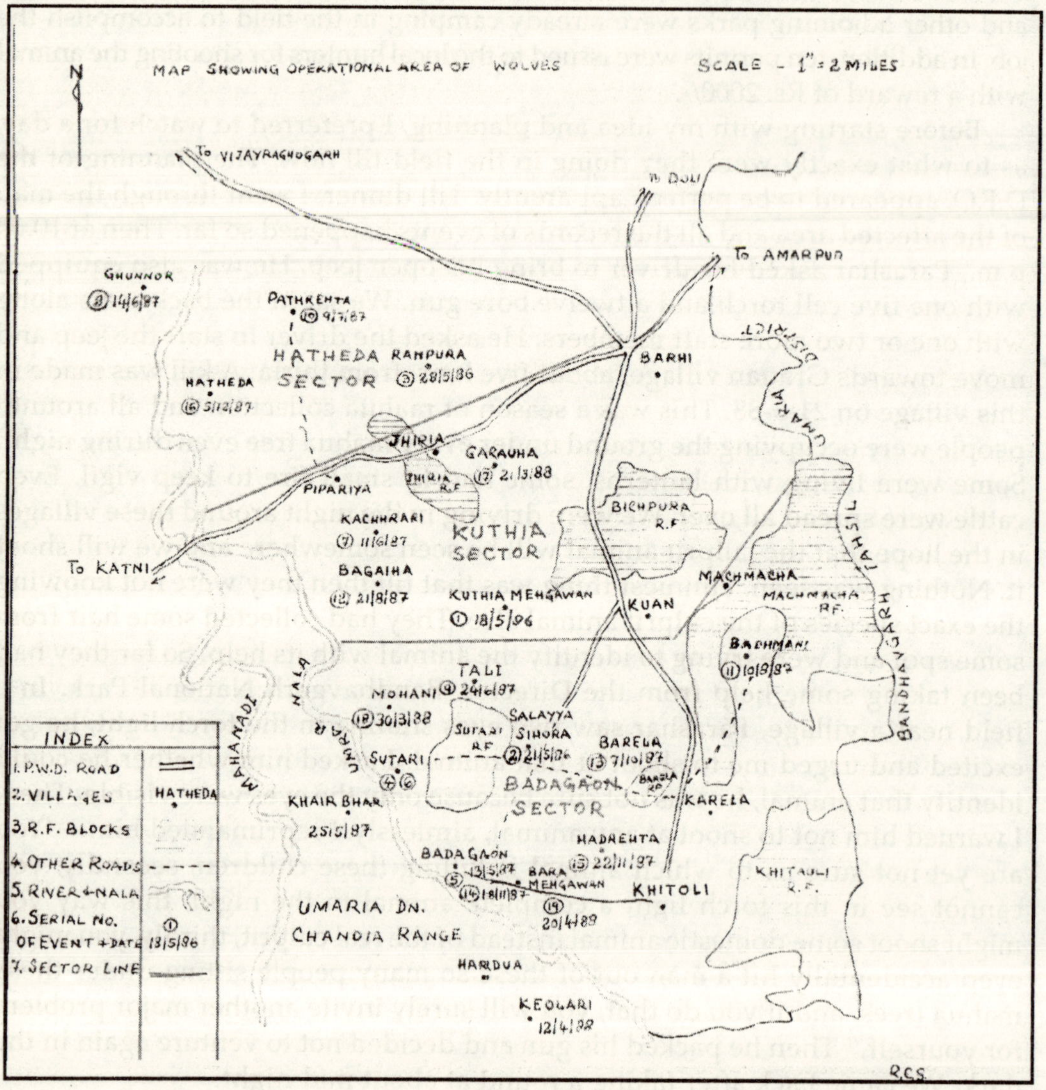

Fig. 7.1: Map Showing Operational Area of Childlifting Wolves

Next day, we came again at Bagaia and as we entered the nala, locally known as Maryadganga, we saw fresh pugmarks of an animal belonging to the dog family, though the pug mark revealed that it was certainly bigger than any dog. I was sure that it was none other than a wolf. We made plaster cast prints of the pug marks. When we came to Bagaia we were informed that a cowherd had seen a wolf in Umrar river also. Another man had seen a wolf near Bagaia on 8-4-88. We immediately rushed to village Loharwara, made a beating party to beat in the Maryadganga nala from its origin it to its last point, but nothing came out of this exercise. By now we were certain that the animal taking toll of the children was a wolf, we also now knew that it wouldn't be possible to see this animal in the dark night and shoot at it with a gun in this vast area with mahua collectors and cattle moving all over. The wolf being a member of the dog family needs a lot of water to drink during summer, and also a lot of shade at the noon hours. As the wolf live in pack I thought that they were more likely to hide in the Ipomea bushes on the banks of these nalas during the day time, where they also had plenty of water to quench their thirst. Usually at dusk, the wolves came out to search and pursue their victims. Their dens were not known so far. Therefore, laced with this behavioural logic we changed our entire strategy; no more aimless night patrolling by different parties. They were instead instructed to include some villagers also in the different parties. The team leaders were to have a gun each and others were to carry sticks. They were asked to start beating the bushes on both the banks of nalas simultaneously, starting from the origin and then covering the entire length. Various nalas of the area were divided amongst these parties and they were supposed to cover all in a days time. I was quite hopeful that the culprit wolves would be caught and killed by these beating parties soon. They were instructed to kill any wolf coming out of these bushes with the help of their sticks or the gun whichever was possible and not any other animal.

From next day, i.e. 10-4-88 our parties were beating the bushes along nalas and we were making further enquiries from the villagers. We covered Barhi, Salaia, Mohni, Bagaia, Nadawan, Pathreta, Singodi and Suddi-Basadi. In two days beating, they got many animals out from these bushes, such as Fox, Rabbits, Jackals but not the wolf. During our enquiry we noticed one thing that after all these cases of killings in various villages, the culprit animal was moving in a particular direction. As if some nuclear spot was there, may be its den, which was not known to any body by then. Again a woman had been reported to have seen a wolf near Maryadganga in village Bagaia. The beating parties were asked to continue the process and we took a break to finish some pending official works and also to wait for some break through by our parties.

On 18-4-88, there was news that a girl of about 10 years age was dragged by the wolf in village Salaia-Sihora, but was saved. On next day we rushed to the field again and halted at Jhiria. Next day I enquired into the incidence in detail. Actually this girl, by name Gauribai, was getting married and the "*Baarat*" had already come to their house. This house was also located in the extreme southern end of the village. A small river, Halphal was flowing just adjacent to it. In the night when everyone fell asleep, a wolf came and lifted the bride, who was sleeping near her father and started dragging her towards the river. As she screamed, everybody got up and ran towards river. By then the wolf had already moved about 20′ distance from the house, but as the luck would have it, she was saved with very little injury. The wolf left her and moved into the Halphal river. Immediately we moved to inspect the river and we found a number of pug marks of the wolves. The entire river bed was full of such marks, which showed that these animals were frequenting this river regularly. Even our patrolling party had seen a wolf in this river bed. I instructed to erect six hides on the left bank of the river at three turning points. Got all the old pug marks erased. Myself, Dr. Kotwal and other staff occupied each hide with guns and sat till it was dark but with no luck.

On 21-4-88, we again sat in the hides from six in the morning, with the hope that the wolves would certainly come to their favourite river. At about 3.00 p.m., we received a message that a child was lifted and eaten in the village Bara Mehgawan in the previous night. Leaving other party members in their hides, Dr. Kotwal and I immediately rushed to Bara Mehgawan. We reached at 4.00 p.m., the mother of the ill fated child Dhaniram was in a state of shock. We consoled and promised her to do our best in searching and killing the animal. Their house was also in the last corner of the village. Like other villagers in the area, despite so much heat inside, were sleeping inside with closed doors and windows. At mid-night, the mother got up to go out and ease herself. She opened the door, in the centre of which a lantern was hung for the light. As she came out in the courtyard, on her left in the shade she saw an animal (on the other side a few domestic cattle were standing). She thought it to be a village dog only and went straight to the outer door and out. She left her 2 year old son alone on the bed unattended. As she returned after a few minutes, she saw the son missing from the bed. She again rushed out and saw the animal moving out of the courtyard with her son in its mouth. She started screaming and shouting for help. All family members and other villagers gathered and followed the animal in the field but could not locate it in the darkness. About a furlong away after the field, there was a small nala. The banks of the nala were little bushy and when we went to the field nearest to this nala, we were shocked to see the pathetic scene. The entire field was splattered with blood of the child and in the centre were lying two small rib bones and a silver bangle which was worn by the child. The scene clearly indicated that it was not a single animal and this job was done by two or may be more animals. No other body parts could be seen any where, perhaps they ate every part of the tender body. As the day was setting, we took a quick search in the nala and other connecting nalas, in the hope of finding the culprit. There was no success, excepting that we flushed out a few foxes, rabbits, etc. again. I gave further instructions to the staff to be vigilant and came back to our camp at Jhiria. Later, the staff while sitting in the hides saw two wolves, shot at them but without any success.

Dr. Kotwal and I were really worried. It was actually very difficult to face the bereaved parents and the villagers. We are usually made to listen to a lot of bad words and taunts, when we are not able to control such happenings.

Next morning in the North East of Salaia village, a few women were collecting mahua flowers. It was just dawn; they saw a dog like animal coming in their direction with a round object in its mouth. When it came a little closer they could see the small head of the deceased child. Immediately they chased and shouted at the animal, it left the head and ran away. We got this information, while we were sitting at the hide in Halphal river. We rushed to Bagaia and were really sad to see the child's severed head. It was really a beautiful child. The head was complete as if chopped off from rest of the body. We decided to use this head as bait and sit on "*Machans*" with guns and take a chance. It was really a tough task to convince the parents to let the head be used as a bait. But the brave parents agreed to give the head for one night only.

We moved to the spot, where this head was left by the wolf (now there was no doubt that this culprit was a wolf). We decided to fasten the head to the ground after wrapping it in a net. Two "*machans*" were erected, one on either side of the head on two Mahua trees. It was almost sun set by the time we completed our "*machans*". By 7.30 p.m. Dr. Kotwal and I occupied the opposite "*machans*". The head was clearly visible in the open space. It was a very windy night, the branches of the trees were swaying too much. Still, we kept on sticking to our positions with our eyes constantly fixed on the head on the ground below. We were praying God to send us that wolf, so that we could free these hapless villagers of this menace, as early as possible. But the animal did not turn up till as late as 2.30–3.00 a.m. Then we left all hope of getting it. We knew that wolves are very cunning and clever also and this pack was particularly smart.

The wolves must have watched us erecting these "*machans*" and doing other activities from a distance in the evening and must have gone away to avoid us. At last we called off our operation at 3.00 a.m. and came back to our camp and returned the head to the parents for cremation.

We sat again with our heads down thinking of our next strategy. Now two most important things which were clear that it was a pair of wolves and as and when they killed a child the remains were carried in one particular direction, most probably towards its den. We decided now to collect about 400–500 persons from the affected villages with sticks and make a huge circle, surrounding an approximate focal point, where we suspected the den might be located. Then beaters, would be beating every bush and searching for animal or its den. I sent message about our new plan to the villagers of Mohni, Mehgawan, Surari and Bara Gaon and waited.

Next day, beating was conducted in about three-kilometre radius. The beaters were asked to keep distance between them, enough to use their sticks on the animal if found anywhere. They were instructed to kill the wolf and not to let it escape in between two persons. Today we could not get the wolves in this beat but got a big success in finding its den, that too with five pups. It happened like this that when one forest guard with beaters was moving along a dry nala, they found a small hole, about 6" diameter on one bank of the nala. One would have left it, thinking it to be of some reptile or the snake. But then one villager, out of curiosity entered his stick in that hole. He felt some thing soft in it. Then he left the stick like that only, the forest guard and others saw it moving up and down. Now they were sure that some animal was there, it was live and breathing. They all got together and started digging out the hole further with the help of pickaxe and shovel. And then they were rewarded with a glimpse of five 2-3 months old pups of the wolves. The adult wolves were not there; perhaps they were out hunting or might have escaped from some other route. It was really a big success and we hoped to get the real culprits very soon, with the help of these pups. Another such den was discovered and smoked, but it was empty.

I fed these pups with half boiled eggs and minced chicken meat. By evening, we were again there at the den. We kept two pups in a small cage (that of Parrot bird) then put it in the big trap cage with drop shutter, which was planted near the den. We thought that the pups will definitely whine for their parents, but will not be able to escape and run away in the night. We put even a gin trap on the entrance of the den. We were really very hopeful to get them this time. Next morning when we came to the spot, we were amazed to see that yes! the adult wolves had come there, but never entered either the den or the drop cage. Instead, they dug all around, as if were trying to dig another tunnel to reach their pups. It spoke of their cunningness and intelligence. We brought back the pups in the day time, again fed them. They were very playful and accepted food freely. Again we repeated the same thing but they were not coming to our traps. We decided to repeat a few more times so that they some how, lose their patience and are trapped alive.

Next day on 24-4-88, I came back to Jabalpur to attend some urgent work in my office. After two days, I came to know that one of the pair, a female wolf was killed by a villager with a stick and the other male was found dead near the trap cage, probably poisoned by the staff. May be it was an unethical end of the beast, but that was the demand of the time. That is how the menace of those child lifters was tackled and after that we never heard of wolves in that area. The pups were first reared by field staff of D.F.O. But three of the pups died in the course of fifteen days time and then other two were sent to Van Vihar Zoo, Bhopal, one of them could see to the adulthood in the zoo. During this period I came to know that the villagers had killed one or two wolves earlier also. Perhaps the gap in the incidences was due to that only, may be that by the time pups (in the habit of eating human flesh) reached adulthood they acquired the man-eating traits of their parents. But in this last episode time all the pups were also eliminated along with the adults, so there was no other incidence thereafter.

It was a great achievement of the D.F.O., Jabalpur and his dedicated staff. They were well organized from the beginning, but lacked skills to match the cunning and intelligent wolves. It was not their fault, they had never dealt with wild animals, and whosoever gave them any idea, they simply followed it. Once they were guided on the right track, they worked very sincerely and could successfully eliminate these child-lifting wolves.

List showing dates and the villages where children were lifted by the wolves.

Sl. No.	*Date*	*Name of the Village*
1.	18-5-86	Kuthia Mehgawan
2.	21-5-86	Slayya-Sihora
3.	28-5-86	Rampura
4.	18-6-86	Sutari
5.	03-5-87	Badagaon
6.	16-5-87	Sutari
7.	11-6-87	Kachhrarhi
8.	14-6-87	Ghunnor
9.	24-6-87	Tali
10.	09-7-87	Pathrehta
11.	10-8-87	Badh
12.	21-8-87	Bagaiha
13.	07-10-87	Barela
14.	18-11-87	Badagaon
15.	22-11-87	Hadrehta
16.	05-12-87	Hatheda
17.	21-3-88	Garhauhan
18.	30-3-88	Mohni
19.	12-4-88	Kewlari
20.	20-4-88	Mehgawan

Episode-VIII

The Child Killer of Supkhar

Yes! I use the word 'Child killer' and not a man-eater, because all the Tigers who kill and eat a man are not necessarily man-eaters. It was 5th August, 1985, we were sitting in our office at Mandla, when we got a message on wireless that a boy was killed by a tiger behind the Forest Rest House, at Supkhar. The body was recovered by the staff; one leg of the boy was eaten by the tiger. Once again Dr. P.C. Kotwal and I rushed to the spot. By the time we reached Supkhar, it was already dark. Those who have seen Supkhar, know that there is no electricity at Supkhar and during rains, even in the day time it becomes gloomy due to overcast sky. The Range Assistant, Saligram Shukla, the Forest Guard and some villagers were there on the spot, looking after the dead body and waiting for the police to come from Garhi. This spot was about two kilometres from the Rest House, on south-west side of Supkhar.

At the rest house, the incidence as told was this—the boy, Lekhan Das, aged 16 years, nephew of the *chaukidar* Suna Lal had come from other village to meet him. In the morning, Lekhan and his cousins, Daya Das and Mangal Singh aged ten and eight years respectively, went out to collect 'peehari', the mushrooms from the Chir Pine plantation, behind the Supkhar forest rest house. After some time, as they were walking back on the main fire line that led to the rest house, an idea came to the mind of Lekhan Das—He asked his friends, "why shall we not make a race competition, you both go straight on this fire line and I would run through this dense forest; let us see who reaches home first". The younger boys ran straight and reached home in half an hour, but their friend Lekhan was not there. They were happy that they had won. They waited for another hour and then started to worry about him. Without telling anybody else, both children came back to the spot, from where they had separated. Here they shouted Lekhan's name twice or thrice, but there was no trace of Lekhan. It was a very dark cloudy day, they felt

Fig. 8.1: Killer Tigress of Supkhar, Bending Her Head to Lift Her Cub

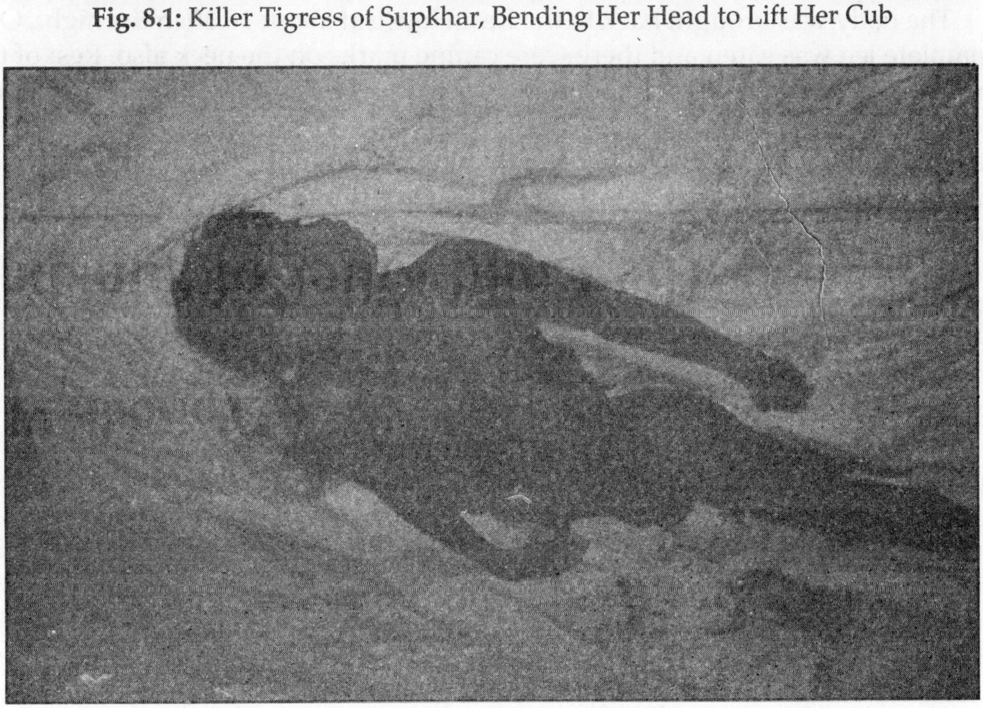

Fig. 8.2: Dead Body of the Boy Lekhan Das, Killed by Tigress

scared and came back and informed the *chaukidar*. Suna Lal and a few more villagers got together and again came to the spot. When they moved a few steps to the direction in which Lekhan had gone, they were shocked to find his umbrella on the ground and a little further his blood stained shorts. They sensed the mishap, and came back running to Supkhar and informed the Range Assistant and Forest Guard regarding the incident.

Once again all of them gathered at the spot with sticks, axes. About five feet ahead from the spot where they had found Lekhan's shorts, they found one foot of the boy. Rest of the body was not there. Suddenly they saw some bushes moving ahead of them. As they followed it, they could see fresh blood dripping on either side on the leaves of the bushes. The tiger was moving about 20' ahead of them, holding the dead body in its mouth. The swinging body, left a trail of blood on the leaves on both sides of the tiger's path. The entire party was shouting loudly and following to shoo away the tiger and get the body of the boy, but the tiger moved on ignoring all the ruckus and noise. It carried the dead body towards south on a small hillock, about 1-1/2 kms. away and then laid it down on the grass. Here villagers made a lot of hue and cry and they could scare away the animal. Once taking charge of the dead body, they lighted a bon fire nearby and kept a watch till police and other officers came. The police reached that spot in the night at about 9.00 p.m. All this while, the tiger was moving around nearby only.

The body was brought back to the Rest House at about 10.30 in the night. One complete leg was eaten and there were canine marks on the neck also. Rest of the body was intact. Whole night, there was activity of the staff around both the rest houses. The dead body was kept in the out house. The Tiger followed back and came behind the rest house and was present there whole night, as Chitals kept on giving alarm calls in the night. I asked the staff not to move in the singles and without lights (torches), just to avoid any other accident. It was our first experience of having a man killer so close. We were also a little scared, thinking that this animal may not sneak in our rest house for picking any of us in lieu of Lekhan Das's body. Anyway, we slept at about 12.30 a.m., after checking all rooms properly, to rise early in the morning. The elephants were called from Kanha and were expected to reach in the night itself.

In the morning, at 6.00, we were again up and on the elephants. Visited the spot and verified the entire incident and could see a glimpse of the tiger also, which vanished soon in the dense bushes. Apparently, there appeared no defect in its movement or behaviour. To see it further, we decided to tie bait near the kill site. The first night, it was not killed. We decided to leave it tethered during day time also. It worked and the bait was killed at about 4.00 p.m. As we went to check, we could clearly see that it was a tigress with small cubs, which could hardly walk. We also saw the tigress shifting its cubs holding in her mouth. Well! That was enough to conclude the reason for the attack. As Lekhan ran for home, the tigress must have been sitting some where in that direction only, with her young cubs. Thinking that Lekhan was coming to harm her cubs, it must have attacked the unfortunate boy. Once he was dead, ate a part of his body as a normal kill or prey. Perhaps it was not intentional attack on human being, as she never repeated again.

Now it was very necessary to take her away from the premises of the Rest houses. Next day again we tied a bait and also moved in the entire area of her movement. As we reached that small hillock, where she had carried the dead body, we found that under thick bushes there were skeletons of so many animals, scattered here and there. It showed that whichever animal she killed, she used to drag it to this hillock and then eat it here. It was actually a home of hers. Our Field Director, Mr. S. B. Lowalekar, Dr. P.C. Kotwal and myself were on three different elephants, mine was the last in row. Suddenly I saw that 'she' the tigress was walking on the heels of my elephant. As I saw it, I asked the mahaut to stop and turn. Others also stopped. On this she jumped and ran away. A young and beautiful tigress. All of us could see her closely, very normal walking, no injury of any type. The only thing which mattered was why she was walking so close to my elephant. What I envisaged was that elephants were never brought in Supkhar till then and this tigress must never have seen any before that day. When we were moving in her home on elephants, she must have become curious to see such huge animals and must have come closer to investigate the reason of our visit. But at any time, she did not show any erratic behaviour.

After that we issued instructions not to enter that side of the forest, be watchful, move in groups, etc. By way of shifting baiting sites away from R.H., we could localize this tigress on hill side in about a month's time. There was no man killing thereafter. Although this tigress was seen by the Range Officer, Udaybhan Singh a number of times on road and P.W.D. labour working on the road, she never charged anybody, though she used to sit and watch them for hours at a time.

Episode-IX

The Man-killer of Ari Village

Ari is a small village on Seoni-Katangi road, in Seoni district of Madhya Pradesh. The distance from district H.Q. is about 30 kms. I was working in Kanha National Park as Deputy Director. On 8-10-79 D.F.O., South Seoni Division (once again my friend Mr. K.K. Parashar) rang up and informed me that a tiger killed a man in the paddy fields of Ari village and was coming to the village side again for the last two days. People were panicky, so also the District Collector. He requested me to come to Seoni immediately and do the needful.

Next day I reached Seoni and then Ari with my staff, with guns, tranquillizing equipment, trap cage, etc. When I visited the spot where Rafique (Raffoo mian) was killed, I found that it was unusual and a very rare incidence. The man was killed right in the centre of the paddy fields. There were fields and fields all around for at least two kms. radius. When we went into the details, we found that there were poor rains that year and the only water reservoir upstream was left with very little water. All these fields were being irrigated by the water discharged from this very dam. All these villagers knew that water in the reservoir was going to exhaust in the next two to three days, so everybody wanted to irrigate and take maximum use of this last water. In this competition, they were out in the field in the night itself. They were sleeping for very little and again by twelve mid-night or so, used to come to their fields. When we inspected the entire forest nearby, there was no herbivore species or the prey base at all. All deer family and the others were finished, excepting a few Wild boars. A full grown Tiger was there, but no prey base sufficient for its survival. And this was the season, when most of these wild boars also come to the fields to feed on the crops. One of the villagers lazy Sewakram, got up late and reached his field at about 6.00 in the morning. Suddenly he was charged by a tiger hiding in his field only. The fields were very wet and muddy, which restricted the movement of this tiger also. On seeing it and hearing

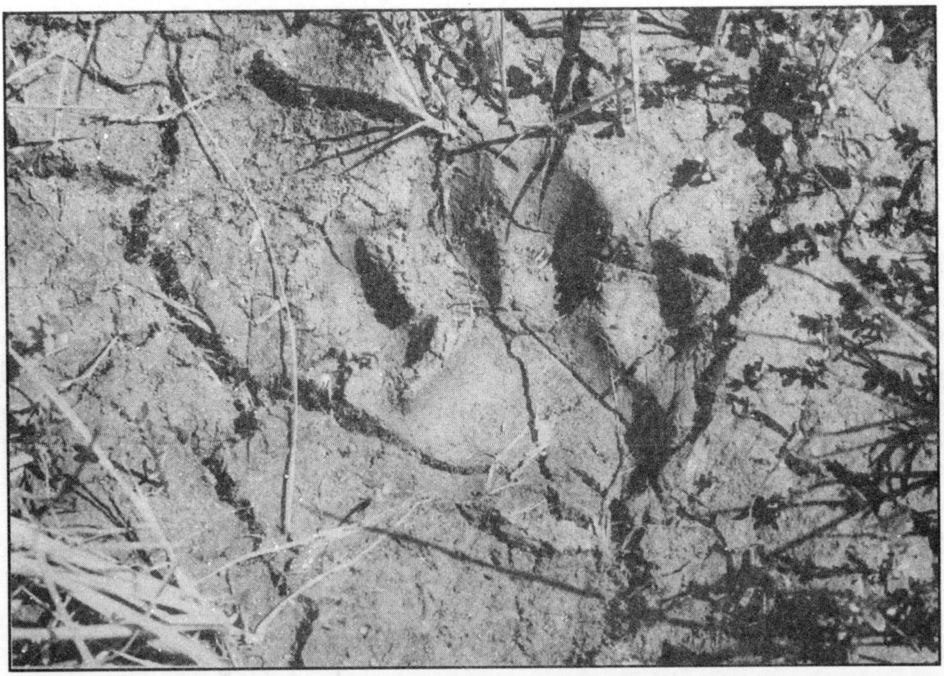

Fig. 9.1: Tiger's Pugmark in Paddy Field, Ari

Fig. 9.2: Team Investigating at Paddy Fields, Ari

its growl, this fellow ran with heels over his head and came back to the village, sweating and trembling. As he said that a tiger was there in his fields, nobody was there to believe him. But when he insisted on it, a young man named Rafique (Raffoo mian) closed his 'Pan' shop and said "come with me, I will show you that it is a dog and not a tiger." Two three more youngsters also joined him. This Pawar also accompanied them up to initial small distance. A group of other 10-15 persons also started following them, but keeping a distance from the first. The adjacent field was a fallow land with no crop in it. Therefore, people had made a footpath on it. All these fields had "Arhar" crop on the bunds around the field and paddy in the centre. "Arhar" was about 2-1/2 'tall and paddy around 2' tall. As they were approaching Sewakram's field, the owner slowed down his pace. He was telling them the exact spot of tiger from a distance behind, moving his hands and fingers. These three boys were moving on the footpath, passing just adjacent to the bund of Sewakram's field. Raffoo was leading in a boasting posture. The tiger was sitting on the bund and hiding in Arhar. As they crossed over at a distance of hardly five to ten feet, the tiger growled to warn them. On hearing this, Raffoo looked back at the tiger and pointing at it shouted "*yeh raha sher*" (here is the tiger). As he did this the tiger felt offended and charged with a leap on Raffoo mian. Raffoo fell down, tiger's one forefoot on his chest and one hind foot on his abdomen. The tiger did not catch him with its mouth. All were spellbound and for a few moments did not know what to do? Then those two friends of Raffoo who had accompanied him lifted a few earthen balls and threw it on the tiger, with loud shouts. Even the tiger was perplexed and was perhaps in a shock. On getting hit with the earthen balls, it instead of attacking them started running towards the forest. It had taken such a long leaps which were 15-20' at places and its feet going so deep in the irrigated muddy fields. It did not turn back and see even once, as if it was in a hurry to reach the forest somehow.

Raffoo was hurt badly, his abdomen opened up with alimentary canal out, four ribs were broken and was immediately shifted to the District Hospital at Seoni. But he could not reach Seoni alive and succumbed to his injuries on way to Seoni. A brave but foolish boy was dead. The entire village was terrified with this incidence. Sewakram, the field owner became hysterical. After that, he started complaining to have seen the tiger daily at different places around the village. That was the reason why was I called there. I verified at different spots told by him, but no signs of tigers visit could be found. Third day, while we were still camping at Ari, he informed that a tiger was again there in the field beyond canal and he heard its calls at about 12.30 noon. It was unbelievable, but then at 3.30 p.m. a police inspector also supported his version and even he was supposed to have heard its call in the field, across canal. He took me to show the tiger from the top of a Babool tree standing in another field. From the top of the tree, he was pointing out at a bund, where the tiger was supposed to be hiding. The sun was about to set, so I had no choice but to go on the spot on foot. By now, I was having a feeling that this tiger had killed Raffoo, accidentally and was gone into the deep forest and this Sewakram was only mesmerized by the incidence and mentally disturbed. Immediately I took my party and rifle with me and went straight to the spot. Sewakram was also with us. Yes, there was no trace of any tiger anywhere. Now he was convinced that it was his imagination only. Actually that night, this tiger had followed a wild boar to kill it and came after it right up to Sewakram's field. The boar somehow escaped and as tiger might have decided to go back, must have heard people (human voices) all around in the fields, who had come to irrigate their fields in the night itself. So this tiger got trapped in this field and stayed out till morning, when this Sewakram came to his field. Because he came very close to tiger in his field, the tiger growled and charged in self-defence. And then Raffoo mian also took liberty in approaching very near and pointing at it aggravated the situation. The tiger never wanted to hurt any man and after this incidence realized its mistake and ran straight to the forest, ignoring so many people in all the fields around and that too in broad day light. It was never a man-eater to be and did never kill any person again. I convinced the Collector also and after discussions with the C.W.L.W., who also came to Ari, I came back to Mandla.

Therefore, any man killing by a tiger must be studied thoroughly and not named a 'man-eater' till it is really a man-eater.

Episode-X

The Wounded Leopard of Ukua

One morning in 1979, we got a message from D.F.O., North Balaghat Division, that a Leopard had become dangerous to human beings near village Ukua of Baihar tahsil of Balaghat district. It had attacked and injured five persons, who were rushed to the District Hospital at Balaghat for treatment. The animal was still in Ukua. Due to rains there was a lot of under growth and greenery, where an animal could hide itself easily. The then Director, Kanha Tiger Reserve, Mr. H.S. Panwar, Dr. P.C. Kotwal, Mr. M.P. Chako, R.O. Kanha and myself immediately packed up our equipment and started off to Baihar. A few days earlier, we had an intensive training on tranquillizing, by Dr. Weisner from Helbrenn Zoo, Germany. We picked up the Tele-inject air gun for the purpose and we all were very excited, this being the first ever tranquillizing experience in the field with a problem animal. At Baihar we found that people from all over, were rushing to that village, in buses, trucks, tractors and by whatever mode of transport, they were getting. When we reached Ukua, it was around 12.00 noon and around five hundred people were surrounding a small open ground, in between houses. It was like a 'mela'. We were told that the leopard was hiding in the distal corner of that open ground in Chakoda bushes. It was not at all visible. The people all around were shouting and some of them pelting stones in that direction.

The first thing was to calm down the mob, which was very difficult. They were in such a large number and there was risk of them being hurt either by our gun or the leopard also. After some efforts, we decided to go ahead with our operation as we were losing time and the number of people collecting there was also increasing. On southern side, where it was hiding, was a bamboo fencing to the kitchen garden of a house, in which maize was growing. On west was also a small fencing which was covering another small open area. So we decided to climb the thatched roof of that house (myself and Mr. Panwar, with tranquillizing gun, from where we could fire the dart easily, once the leopard was made visible. Mr. Chacko stood on the entrance with .315 rifle to take a cover shot in case of any emergency. Dr. Kotwal came with a covered and closed jeep from eastern side to flush out the leopard. As the jeep pressed on to that comer, the leopard jumped into the kitchen garden and sat under the maize plants, which were around 3′ tall. As it jumped and was visible to the people, they started shouting again and were trying to close in. Those who have used such tranquillizing guns, know that we have to fill up air with a foot pump to the required pressure, as per distance and weight of the dart. There on the sloping thatch roof, I was not finding any place to keep the foot pump and use it. With great difficulty we could do it. Mr. Panwar took the aim and fired, but unfortunately it hit a wooden pole and not the leopard. The leopard got disturbed and again jumped out of that fencing into the next opening. Here, many people started running after it despite our warning them. Suddenly, the leopard turned back and attacked three more persons with its claws. Then only people moved back. In Balaghat district, most of the village houses are having a huge main opening with no door in it. Even bullock-cart can also enter through it. They are mostly '*kacha*' mud houses. One such mud house was there in front of this open land. The leopard started running towards that house, just to avoid that crowd which was still chasing it, keeping little distance. We also jumped down and followed it. In this particular house, there was a small enclosure made of bamboo walls on right side of the opening. This enclosure was having a small bamboo door (*khatka*) also. It also had a false roof of loose bamboos on it.

As the leopard ran towards it, two boys of the age of 18-19 years, who were present there, quickly climbed on the roof of that enclosure. The door (*khatka*) was already open, the leopard immediately entered this enclosure, instead of going any further. Mr. Panwar again prepared his gun and as we moved ahead, we saw that the leopard was sitting in the enclosure and facing our side only. It was getting disturbed on seeing anybody coming to that house and was getting furious. I told him that it would not be possible to dart in such conditions. After pushing the crowd away, we came to the side wall of the house and started thinking of other alternatives. The first thing, when we saw the leopard in the enclosure and the boys on its roof, we asked them to close the door, if possible. Yes! those brave boys did it and the leopard was temporarily trapped inside. Actually it was concentrating on the human beings, coming from the front only and was almost unaware as to two persons were sitting just on its head. There were no windows or other openings on the road side. We did not know much about the plan of the house. And after some time, we saw two young chaps suggesting us a route to the enclosure. They were the same boys, who were sitting on the roof of the enclosure. Very smartly and bravely they escaped through a hole, meant for ventilation for a cattle room (*maveshi ki saar*), which was located just above their head, where they were sitting. Just adjacent to the wall of this enclosure, was a big, 25′ long and 12′ wide room, which was being used to keep cattle in the night, locally known as '*Saar*'. Besides an opening door from the courtyard, it had a small round opening of about 2.5′ diameter, being used as a ventilator. It was located at a height, just above the height of the roof of the bamboo enclosure, in which the leopard was sitting. From a back door, myself and Dr. Kotwal entered this '*saar*' and then climbed to this ventilator. Somehow, we entered this small hole and crossed over to the roof of the enclosure (especially Dr. Kotwal), quietly, without disturbing the leopard. It was so silent move that even that leopard could not know our arrival on its head. The step was very risky. Now filling air in the gun was also required to be very silent. Mr. Panwar and the other staff were helping us by diverting leopards attention towards them only. Through these loose bamboos of the roof, I darted the leopard. It was a perfect shot at such a short distance and that too right above the animal. We succeeded in getting it down in another 5-6 minutes time. Brought the leopard to Baihar, weighed it at a flour mill (till then we did not have a spring balance and the weighing platform with us), put it in a transportation cage which was made of welded wire mesh and a wooden frame. On our way back to Kanha, it came back to its senses. A huge male leopard it was, a beautiful animal indeed. It was annoyed having been caught and trapped and was roaring so loudly. Every now and then it was shaking the cage and the jeep as if trying to open the cage and coming out.

Next morning when we saw it, it had already wounded its muzzle by hitting against the wire mesh. It was again tranquillized for treatment. We found that it had a hole in the abdomen also, from which blood was oozing out. The wounds were cleaned and suitable medicines were applied externally. Long acting antiseptic injections were also given by Dr. Mandlekar, a veterinary officer from Mandla. But by 10.30 p.m. it died also. During post mortem, we found that a bullet had entered its abdomen and had lodged in its liver, damaging most of its internal organs. Obviously, somebody had fired on it to kill, but was instead injured and so attacked many persons in a revengeful behaviour and finally, succumbed to its injuries.

We were lucky that we succeeded in getting this animal without much harm to public also. But we learnt one thing that one must take police along with him to control the mob in such situations. Secondly, the transportation cage for cats at especially, should not be open, but a closed and a blind cage of plywood will not disturb the animal. In such cages, the animal cannot see any person handling it and, hence, are calm during journey. The cage has to have a three centimetre gap between the claddings of the roof, bottom and the four sides for ventilation of the cage. The wooden claddings should be inside the iron frame, so that the animal does not injure its head or its claws in attempts to break free.

The leopard is in grass dump.

A hunting jeep was brought from the opposite sid

Some trials were done from the roof of
adjoining hut.

But the leopard ran away towards other houses,
hurting few persons.

It takes shelter in a bamboo shed, in a house.

The leopard is sitting in a bamboo shed.

The door of shed is being closed by the persons already sitting on the roof.

The leopard was trapped now.

Through the ventilator we came over the roof and shots were made from the slits, and it was gone.

Episode-XI

The Gaur that Strayed into the Villages

It was morning of 5-1-86, when our Field Director, Mr. Lowlekar called me and Dr. Kotwal to his residence. Some urgent matter was to be discussed. When we entered the drawing room, he was already talking to Conservator of Forest, Balaghat circle on phone. After the talk was completed, we were told that a Gaur (the Indian Bison) had strayed into some 2-3 villages of Balaghat district near Katangi. It had killed one man and injured badly three women and one bullock and was still hiding in one of the sugar cane fields. It was on killing spree and help to tranquillize it, was immediately required. By then, we had tranquillized a number of animals of cat and deer family, but never a bovine. We were experienced in handling cats and deer after it was doped, but never a bovine and as large animal as a Gaur.

As we discussed, we were facing two major problems. Firstly, that Katangi was quite far and our elephants could not reach there soon, so how to approach such an erratic and powerful animal with adequate safety. Secondly, if ever we approach safely and are able to tranquillize the animal, what next. We did not have a large cage enough to keep a Gaur sized animal in it. In open truck, if we think of bringing this animal to the forest back, how to pick it up and load it safely. After a lot of thinking, we decided not to venture out on this mission, instead we informed them to get the animal shot with the help of police department, after seeking due permission from the Chief Wildlife Warden. As we were still sitting there, suddenly phone came from the Additional Chief Wildlife Warden, from Bhopal, who ordered us to proceed immediately to the spot with whatever equipment we had and tranquillize the animal or otherwise inform the conditions as may be. We had no choice.

In the afternoon, I came to Kanha and readied the equipment and then halted at Mukki. I and Dr. Kotwal were to stay in the wooden Rest House (the Log Hut). It was coldest night and the temperature recorded was 2° centigrade. It was windy

Fig. 11.1: The Site, Where Gaur Dragged and Injured Three Women

Fig. 11.2: The Victim Bullock, Which was also Attacked by Gaur

Fig. 11.3: Site at which a Man was killed by the Gaur

also, whole night we were trying to sleep but we were cold up to bones inside, no heater, no fire place. Ultimately, got up at 4.30 a.m., woke up our Field Director and by 5.30 we preceded for Katangi. By about 7.00 a.m., we were there at Katangi, caught hold of Range Officer and proceeded to village Badagaon after a cup of tea. We were taken to a sugar cane field, in which the Gaur was still supposed to be hiding. It was around 100 mts. by 100 mts. field with standing crop of tall sugar cane and on three sides of it was open fallow land (recently tractor ploughed field). The staff and the villagers were very sure that the animal was still there in the sugar cane. We brought the jeep right up to the field. We could not find any hoof marks or cow dung around this field. We were very cautious as we knew that if it charged our jeep also, it could turn it upside down. From Katangi, we got some quantity of crackers also. It was a bright day, so put villagers and the staff all around, but at a safe distance and instructed them to keep away from its route of escape, not to fall on it or to follow if it came out of the field. Then we threw some cracker bombs in side the field. It burst so loudly, but there was no movement inside the field. We tried again covering other side of the field, but again of no avail. Now we were sure that there was no animal inside the field or if at all it was there, it could not move. So we took our rifles for self-defence and entered the field. Yes! There was no animal whatsoever. As all of the fields around were tractorised, we could not find any hoof marks. The villagers and the staff had surely seen it entering this field, but then it must have escaped to the forest in the darkness of night, when disturbance must have ceased in the night.

As people told us, this animal was first seen near village Atri, drinking water in a nala at dawn. Some mischievous boys on seeing it, surrounded it and started shouting and petting stones on it. The poor animal started running here and there, wherever it found any opening, but could not run towards the forest. More and more people gathered and started chasing it. While running for life, a bullock came in the way which was then charged by the Gaur. One horn of Gaur entered its abdomen. The bullock did not die and was bandaged by the villagers. When we saw, it could not stand on its feet. Now this animal (Gaur) started running towards village Nandsara. Here a man came in its way, who was taken on its horns and thrown in the air. Before he came down to the ground, it was again taken on horns and now he was dead. After this, this Gaur sat in a grove of trees. But the villagers, who were little afraid now, approached again and started throwing stones. It got furious, got up and started running on the back side of a row of the houses. These three houses were having open backyard and the three women of the houses were cooking meals in their respective houses. On hearing this hue and cry, as they got up and stood in their yards, this Gaur charged one woman first, trampled and dragged her for some distance, then second and the third woman. These poor ladies were very badly trampled and injured and were rushed to the District Hospital at Balaghat.

From this village, it came to Badagaon village and lodged itself in this sugar cane field. As the things are, these bovines are never known to be man killers (habitual). After all they are powerful wild animals and any irritation by human beings is taken to be offensive and they charge only in self-defence. Therefore, in all such cases, if any wild animal strays into the villages/townships, it can easily be sent back to forest. Keeping forest side open, it can be driven back slowly with a silent drive by a small group of persons without disturbing or irritating much to the animal. In such drives we should not use drums, trumpets, or much shouting, on the other hand, keeping a safe distance beating bush or ground with sticks, once/twice and then wait. Again repeat after some time. This way the animal is not agitated and slowly walks back to the forest without harming anybody. It must never be surrounded from all sides. Practically, it is very difficult as the people do not understand the behaviour of these wild animals and become rowdy in big mob formations. Therefore, police must be called on the spot in order to control the mob. People listen to them only and not the forest officials. In almost all such cases, if the animal is unable to go back, due to mob surrounding them, they escape and rush back to the forest, only in the darkness of night, when all people break the cordon and go back to sleep.

Only in case of established man-eating cats, wolves or sometimes hyenas, one has to take different steps to eliminate such animals. They may not even behave in this manner at all.

Episode-XII

'Sagar'—The Tiger of Teetarpani

On 5-5-87, a message was received from Conservator of Forest, Sagar Circle, that a huge Tiger fell in side a dry well at a village near Teetarpani. It was alive and could not come out unless tranquillized and lifted out. Our Field Director, Mr. Lowalekar called me and asked me to proceed immediately. As the area was unknown to me, Mr. A.S. Parihar, the then Park Interpretation Officer, who was earlier D.F.O. Nauradehi Sanctuary at Sagar was also sent with me to guide the way, so that we could reach the spot at the earliest. Immediately a rescue team was ready with cage and equipments. The last minute instruction was not to bring the animal (tiger) to Kanha under any circumstances. The reason was that all our cages at Kanha were already occupied by tigers and panthers rescued from other areas. Secondly, it was very costly and difficult to arrange for their feed daily at Kanha and also to render treatment.

We started off from Mandla at about 6.00 p.m. After driving for almost whole night, we reached Teetarpani at 6.00 a.m., via Jabalpur, Patan, Tendukhera, etc. Mr. Parihar told me that there was a P.W.D. Rest House at Teetarpani, where we could fresh ourselves and start our job. But there at Teetarpani, there was an anti-climax. The roof of the entire rest house was removed and was under major repair. Bathrooms were not usable. Therefore, we had to go to the field with our mugs. Had a quick mouth wash and instead of wasting anytime, proceeded to the nearby village where this tiger was trapped in a well. The only local staff, whom we could take with us at this early hour, was Mr. Tiwari A.C.F., who was incidentally inspecting the lots in timber depot at Teetarpani. Earlier he worked as Superintendent at Pachmarhi and Sitanadi sanctuaries. On the spot, we reached at about 7.30 a.m. There was nobody, no rush, no crowd. It was the best time and best atmosphere to do our job.

Fig. 12.1: Sagar, the Tiger in the Well with Live Goat

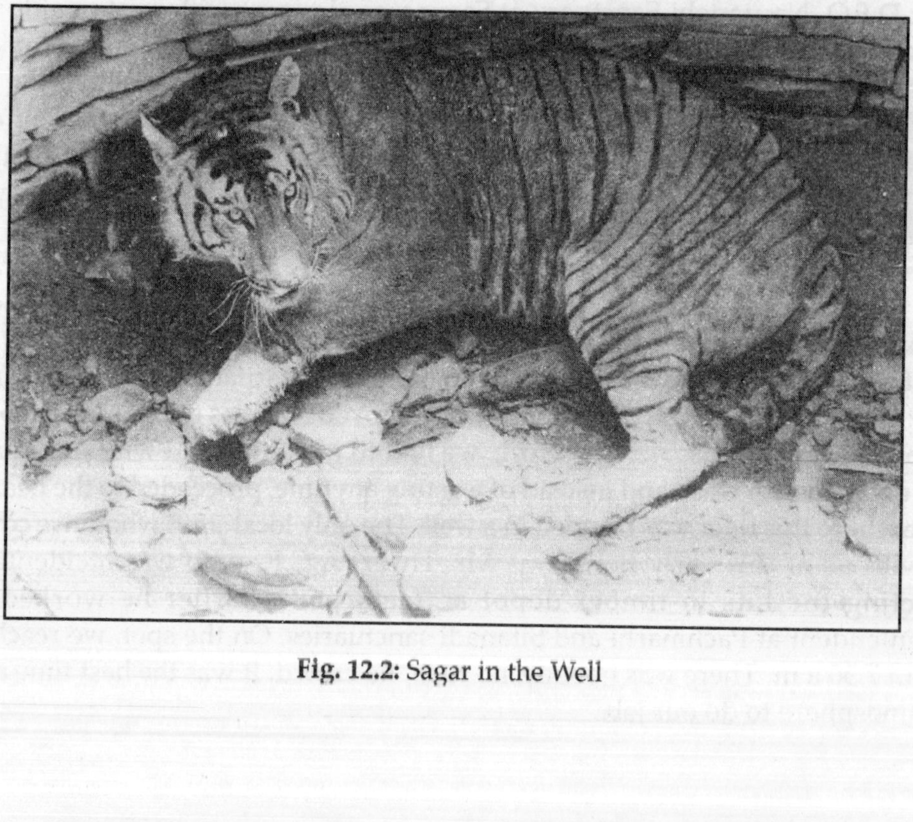

Fig. 12.2: Sagar in the Well

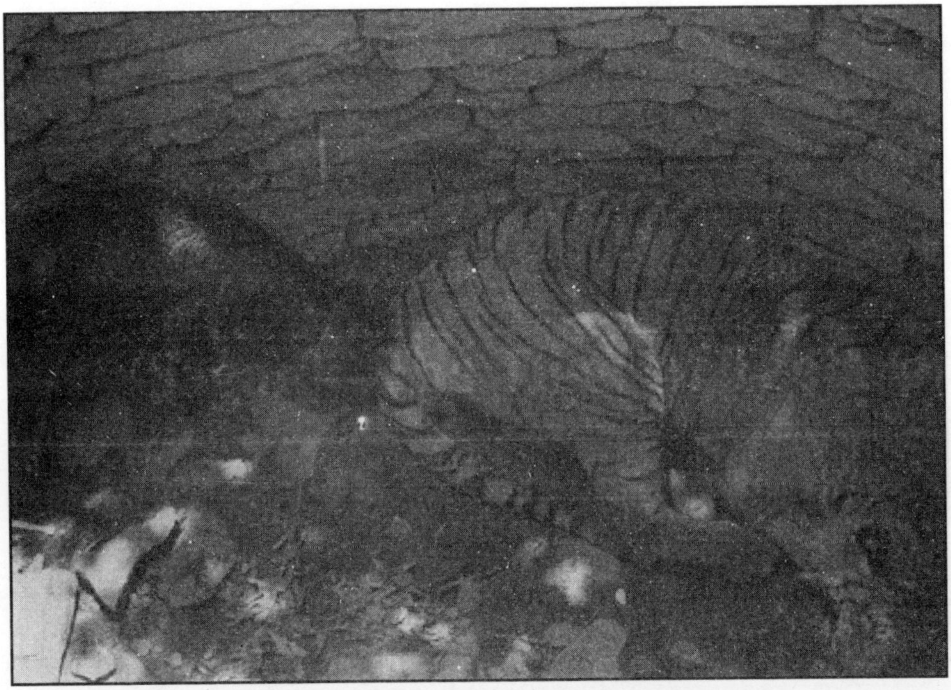

Fig. 12.3: The Goat with the Tiger in the Well, Sniffing at it

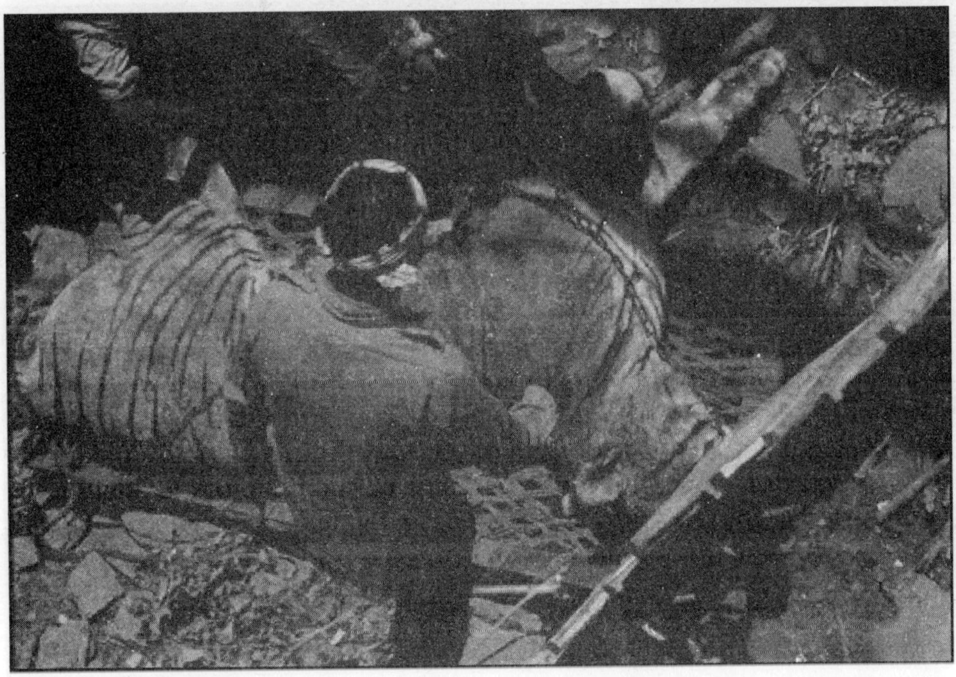

Fig. 12.4: Manglu Baiga Fixing the Tranquillized Tiger on the Cradle

Fig. 12.5: Tiger 'Sagar' in the Cradle, half way up the Well

Fig. 12.6: The Live and Brave Goat with Officers and Other Staff

Fig. 12.7: Manglu, the Legendary Baiga who Participated in Many Episodes

The well was about 30′ diameter large and 30′ deep also. It was still under construction. Still there was no water in it. The walls were made of loose piled up stones, without any adhesive in it. All stones were of random shape and sharp edges were protruding from almost all stones. There was no parapet wall. The well was located in a field, little away from the main village. Some passerby from some other village came to the well in search of water but were faced with a tiger instead. Immediately they informed the other local villagers and the forest staff. A huge and healthy male tiger was there in the well. On seeing human beings, it got irritated, growled and jumped towards them. People also noticed that a dead wild boar was also inside the well. The tiger was not eating the boar. Perhaps while chasing a wild boar, both of them fell inside well. After some time people from the village downed a live goat to feed the tiger, but neither did it kill nor ate it.

When we saw the tiger, it was very docile and sitting cuddled in the well. Perhaps, it was tired and was thinking about the ways to get out of it. The funniest scene was, when the goat unaware of powers of a tiger was sniffing at it, this lord of the jungle was bundling in itself, as if feeling shy of himself. It was not at all worried about his food or water, but was worried only to get out of this hell (well). The tiger was intermittently looking at us also, just to guess about our activities. The light was perfect, the object (tiger) was sitting in such a pose that its thigh muscles were fully exposed for a perfect target. I prepared two darts of HBM mixture, making a slight change in the proportions of the two ingredient medicines.

Normally, 400 mgs. of Ketamine hydrochloride is mixed with 500 mgs. of Xylaxine hydrochloride in HBM mixture, instead I used 500 mgs. of Ketamine with same quantity of Xylaxine. The dart landed perfectly on the thigh of the tiger. It got up quietly, walked a while along the wall of the well. In this process, the tail of the dart got stuck up in the protruding wall stones. The tiger came back to its original position and sat there. Within 5-7 minutes, it was down. The goat was moving here and there and even sniffing at the bright coloured tail of the dart. We pelted a few pebbles on the tiger to be sure and then lowered our great asset Manglu Baiga into the well. Mr. Tiwari had already arranged a long and strong rope from his timber depot. It was a full grown and very hefty tiger. Now was the problem as to how to lift this tiger up. We used to have a small frame of a cot, without legs, which had four chains hooked to the four corners. It was used to weigh the animals with the help of spring balance. We decide to lower this down along with that long rope. The top of the well was having a small platform, made of wooden poles and bamboos. It was covering about one third of the well and was perhaps used for pulling up earth while digging. First, the tiger was put on the wooden weigh frame and then was pulled up with the rope. It was so heavy that it could be lifted only half way after this the frame was tilting on one side. It was very risky, the tiger could fall from our frame and that could have killed the tiger itself or if fell on Manglu Baiga, he would have been fatally injured. Again we lowered it to the bottom of the well. We were losing time. Generally, once tranquillized, any cat with HBM, it is down for about an hour's time. After that, either we have to give more drug or the animal must be put in a cage before this time is elapsed. It is for our own safety.

We had already lost half an hour and the tiger was still in the well along with Manglu Baiga. This time a rope was wrapped around the tiger and the frame to fasten the animal to its carrier. It was pulled up this time along the wall of the well. But when on the top, two of its four corner chains used to get folded taking the body of the tiger downside. Two or three attempts were made, but all in vain. It was not possible to lift the frame with tiger on its upper side. Fifty minutes passed. Now there was no time left to think. I made the frame tops turvy, bringing the tiger overboard with our weighing frame on the tigers back. Then we changed the position, untied hurriedly. By that time, our tiger started moving its ears. So there was no time left to weigh it or measure it. Immediately it was loaded on to our transportation cage (a blind cage). The live goat was also brought up, a lucky one. The goat was very brave also, no fear of tiger at all. A strange happening.

We came to Teetarpani Rest House, had our meals and rested during the hot hours. But strange enough, our tiger was still sleeping. By about 4.00 p.m., we started for Sagar. Mid way, we found the Conservator, D.F.O.s and other officers rushing towards Teetarpani. They were astonished to see us. They were expecting us to reach Teetarpani now from Mandla, they could never expect that we would travel whole night for this job. All back to Sagar, the tiger cage was kept at

Conservator's bungalow. From C.F's bungalow report was sent to Field Director, Kanha and the C.W.L.W. M.P., Bhopal on phone. The Chief Wildlife warden asked me to take the tiger to Kanha, whereas our Field Director had already instructed me not to do so. The tiger got up at about 7.00 p.m., fully awaken and had good amount of water also.

At the Forest Rest house, Sagar, the success of our mission was celebrated by the Conservator. But myself and Mr. Parihar were all the time worried as to whom to follow. For once we thought of moving back to Kanha, leaving tiger at C.F's bungalow only. Then he would have managed as he liked. The Chief Wildlife Warden had also informed us that he had sent Mr. S.M. Hasan from Bhopal also along with cage and equipment and was on his way. Then we decided to wait for him. In the morning Mr. Hasan also said the same thing that the C.W.L.W. had asked not to bring the tiger to Bhopal. But C.F., Sagar favoured us by telling a lie that C.W.L.W. had agreed in the last evening on phone to take the animal to Bhopal. On hearing this, our friend Hasan did not ask another question, lifted the tiger cage in his truck and left for Bhopal. That is how we could solve such a ticklish problem. Actually, at the time of a lame tiger, which was caught near Kisli, our all permanent cages were full with some cat or the other. Even at that time, when I came to Jabalpur and talked to CWLW to get instructions regarding it, (at that time it was not possible get phone so easily from Mandla), he told me to shoot one of the sick and dying animals and make room for this tiger. But then myself and my Field Director decided to wait for a few days. Till then the tiger remained in the squeeze cage itself. After two days we were astonished to get a written instruction, not to shoot but to wait for a few days more. Had we done it as per telephonic instructions, we would have been in trouble. From Sagar also when I informed the then C.W.L.W. that there was no cage vacant to keep this tiger in, again he asked me to shoot one and make room, but not to send the tiger to Bhopal. Myself and Mr. Parihar were thinking of releasing this tiger in the forest from where it was supposed to have come, but its wrist of left fore foot was injured badly. It was cut and opened almost half of its depth and needed immediate medical attention. So we changed our mind.

Here at Bhopal, it was operated upon and with due medical care from veterinary department, recovered fast and soon became normal. It was a huge tiger that never tolerated man near him for many years and, hence, was never shown to the visitors, for quite long time. It lived long and was even shown to the visitors in Van Vihar. It was sent to Indore zoo on 21-1-1992, where it remained one of the main attractions and lately, it died on 21-7-1998 at about the age of 16 years due to throat and lung infections.

Episode-XIII

The 'Wayward' Tiger of Atri Village

Leopards are known to stray into villages in search of food, such as dogs, goats and poultry. But the tigers are seldom known to have entered the villages, unless they are man-eaters. On 27-5-87, we got a message from C.F. Balaghat that a tiger had entered the village of Atri and was hiding inside the 'hay store' of a farmer's house. It had attacked and injured a girl who had gone to fetch hay to be fed to the cows in the evening. We thought it to be a leopard only, which might have entered the village in search of food, but they were all insisting on it to be a tiger.

My Field Director, Assitant Director Mr. M.P. Chacko and I decided not to waste time. We immediately took the necessary equipment and proceeded for village Atri. We thought of first reaching the spot, assess the situation and then seek local help from the forest staff. The reason was that a tiger could have caused more damage by injuring more human beings; therefore, it was advisable to reach the spot as early as possible. We reached Atri at mid-night about 12.30 a.m. Here we were relieved to see the peaceful atmosphere; almost all the villagers had gone to sleep. One man somehow brought us to that house where the tiger was hiding inside the hay store. This village had got lanes and the people were quite rich. They generally make very big mud houses. In one such lane, where our truck and other vehicles could enter easily, was that house. All the living rooms were on right side of the lane and the hay store was on the left side. The house owner was still awaken and had put one extra bulb in front of the house and was watchfully sitting near it. The hay store was divided into two big rooms. Such stores do not have any doors and only big openings are there in the front side. There are no windows and electricity fittings to avoid any fire hazard from accidental short-circuit and sparking. The house owner told us that his daughter of about 15 years age had gone to the right side room of the hay store, to fetch hay to be fed to the cows with a kerosene lantern in her hand. And suddenly a tiger jumped at her and injured her arm with its claws. But when she started screaming and shouting

The tiger is sitting in a saar, hiding itself in grass

We could not take a shot from the shutter as it could hurt the

We came on the bamboo ceiling
through the vendilator

Light was thrown from the door and shotwas made from
the slit in bamboo ceiling, this way it was done.

the tiger retreated. Later on when more men gathered and went inside to see the animal, it came rushing at them but when it saw a big crowd it entered the other room on left side. Then people brought a huge wooden shutter and closed the entrance of the store. The animal was seen by them and everyone was certain that it was a tiger.

When we flashed light through a small opening of the shutter and searched for the animal, we could locate the animal with great difficulty. The hay store was full of hay, most of which was stacked on about 3' high platform in order to avoid dampness. Even otherwise the surplus hay was there everywhere. In this stacked hay, on one platform there was a cave like opening, in which the tiger was resting. Its head was facing outside and the remaining body was hidden inside. On seeing torch light from us, it turned its head upwards and started staring at us. Its eyes were glittering sharply. We could see the stripes of the face and shoulders also, which confirmed it to be a tiger only. It was a strange sight.

Though the animal was not visible completely, its head showed and was assessed to be a sub-adult of two to two and a half years of age. Its health and other body defects, if any, could not be assessed. Our source of light was only this beam of torchlight that went inside through a small opening. We tried to find out any other opening around this room by moving all around, but there was none. Making another suitable opening in the wall was also not possible, as the walls were 2-3' thick and made of black cotton soil which becomes very hard. The only thing that favoured us was absence of a crowd and a peaceful atmosphere, and we wanted to take advantage of it. We were eager to finish our job before the entire village woke up. We could not dart the animal from the same opening, from where we were throwing flash light on the animal. The reason was that it was lying on one side and looking at the light and the dart could only be aimed at its head, which we did not want to try. This is not the right place to shoot at and the risk of hitting the eyes was high.

At last they showed us two ventilator type openings, about 15' above the ground on the right side of the room, located on the other part of the hay store. These opening were on the upper side of the bamboo ceiling, which covered both the rooms. We thought of entering these ventilators and search for other small openings, from where we might see and dart the animal. Myself and Mr. Chacko called for a long ladder and then somehow crawled in. This was an unknown and risky place where we might have come across rats, insects, lizards or even snakes. But we hardly had any choice. We asked them to throw light on the tiger so that we could search for some opening in the bamboo ceiling, on which we were sitting. This room's ceiling extended over the tiger's room also, crossing over the mud wall partition. Oh! Yes, we could see a streak of light between two bamboos, which was too close to the outer left wall. From here we could see about 2/3 portion of the tiger very clearly, its shoulder fully exposed. But we had no clue how to fire the gun and dart it from such a cramped perch. Keeping the butt of the gun on the right shoulder, we were not able to aim. Yet, I took a chance and put the butt on my left shoulder, sticking to the left outer wall, aimed and for the first and the last time fired with my left hand. We were very lucky to see that our dart landed right in the centre of the shoulder. The tiger was almost unaware of what had happened. It was because, all this time it was looking at the torch light, which might have blinded it temporarily and our dart also came from the top. In five minutes, the tiger was down, we brought it out. It was a sub-adult, quite weak and bony. Perhaps it had no food for many days and had entered the village in search of it. The forest area around these villages are short of prey base and for the big cats, it is very difficult to survive without prey. Earlier also a sub-adult had entered a hut at Pandri-Tikra village on Mandla-Raipur road on 31-10-1986. Both these animals had no external injury as such, but both were found starving.

After taking weight and other measurements, we put the tiger in a transportation cage at about 5.00 a.m. and pushed off to Balaghat. It was a very peaceful operation. When we reached C.F., Balaghat's bungalow and woke him up at about six, he came out rubbing his eyes. He said "you have come so early, all right have a cup of tea; in the mean time I call the D.F.O. and the Range Officer to accompany you to the spot. The tiger is trapped inside a room, so it can't escape and run away". Then we informed him that the tiger was standing out side his bungalow in our cage. He was so astonished that he had no words of praise for us.

Episode-XIV

A False Alarm: The Malajhkhand Tigress

It was 1979, one year had passed for me working in the wildlife field. It was a pleasure working in Kanha with Mr. H.S. Panwar as Field Director. We got many opportunities to work together on animals in distress. On one day Mr. Panwar called me and Dr. Kotwal and said that we had to rush to Malajhkhand, the copper mines in Balaghat district, immediately. "There is a complaint that a tigress with two cubs is roaming in the civilian area for the last fortnight and the residents and the workers all are terrified. It moves in the colony and people have stopped coming out after sunset." Mr. Panwar was down with a fever and, hence, he could not accompany us.

Next day, myself and Dr. Kotwal reached Malajhkhand, contacted the authorities over there. Everybody was talking about this tigress. These mining areas had a number of forest clad hills around it. We interviewed some of the night duty staff, who were supposed to have seen the tigress. They said that she visited almost daily but never harmed anybody. We asked these people individually, as to how did it look and had they seen a tiger earlier. Some had seen tiger in a zoo, some in circus. But there descriptions were raising doubts. The size of the animal was not clear. Almost all fled on the first sight of it. Anyway, we had to search for its pugmarks if it was visiting daily. We walked on all the footpaths leading to the forest, but due to gravel could not see any pugmarks. Whole day we spent around these forested hillocks, but no clue. As the sun was setting, we decided to go back and decide our next step. Then at a place, we could see clearly the pug marks of a hyena, leading to the forest at a distance, we could see two eyes shining, but certainly were not of a tiger.

From Kanha, we informed the details to Mr. Panwar on wireless and discussed about further action. He said that their G.M. was very much worried and we must put more efforts to ascertain the animal and its cause of visit, so that suitable treatment could be done. It is very important area and needed complete investigation. Malajhkhand mines are not very far from Kanha tiger reserve, hardly 25-30 kms. away. Therefore, we decided to take a few elephants and with their help, patrol in the night and comb the forest during day time, to see the animal in question. Next day two of our elephants came with us to Malajhkhand. We were equipped with search lights and the guns for self-defence. We were lodged in the rest house of the mines. Instructions were issued, to all people living in the colonies and the night watchmen to inform any sighting of the tigress at anytime of the night, immediately at our rest house camp. Myself and Dr. Kotwal also decided to patrol the entire affected area on elephants, with search lights.

The first night, neither we saw any tiger nor any information came. During next day time, we combed one side of the forest. Astonishingly, there were no animal in it. No wildlife whatsoever. We were trying to see the tigress in question or its prey base at least. But it was a total blank. Most probably, either the wild animals had left the area due to mining operations and sounds of the machines, or they were kitted by local *shikaries*. Anyway, one more night was there to patrol. This evening, we had good showers also and all ground around was wet. At 11.30 p.m., we arrived at the petrol pump of the mines, which was located away from living area on one corner. It was aloof building and light inside was on. We knew that the night watchman here had seen the so-called tigress 2-3 times earlier also. When I saw inside from the opened window, the man was shaking profusely out of fear. I asked him as to what had happened. With great difficulty he said that he had seen the tigress, five minutes before on that road, leading to the petrol pump. He was coming for duty at the petrol pump, hardly hundred yards before it, suddenly the tigress sitting on one side of the road jumped over his head and landed on the other side of the road. He was on his cycle, quickly he came to his room at the petrol pump and bolted from inside. He was alone. I asked him to open the door and come with us to the exact spot, but he refused to do so. He was afraid even to open the door. I told him that we were standing out side and there was no danger, but he did not budge. Ultimately I put my hand inside and caught hold of his collar and threatened him to break his head if he did not open now. Then he opened the bolt of the door. We assured him not to be afraid, as we had guns and were on the elephants. With a lot of persuasion he came on to my elephant and came to the spot where he was claiming to have come across that tigress. But again there was no trace of either the tigress or any sign of it. It is unbelievable that a tiger would not leave pug marks or any other sign of its presence on wet soil. After a lot of cajoling, I could convince that person that it was his imagination only. He could regain some courage and confidence also. Actually he was working alone at such a secluded place for so many days, then this so-called sighting of a tigress by many people added further fear in his mind and he started seeing this imaginary tigress.

Next day, we combed the remaining parts of the forest area and found no prey base, no signs of any kills, pugmarks or any evidence, except hyena pug marks at one or two places. The night also was totally clueless. Next morning, there was "*wishwakarma pooja*" and some variety entertainment show was being organized by the authorities. We were also invited to the show. Almost all of the "*Sarpanches*" from the surrounding villages were also invited to the show. I availed of this opportunity and called all of them on one side and interviewed them. All of them said that they had not seen any tigress in their villages and that there had been no report of tiger killing a cow or any other cattle during the last 8-10 months time.

Now the picture was becoming clear. A tigress with two growing cubs could not survive in that area, without any prey base. If at all it was there, it was not killing any cattle so far, then how was it surviving without food? No! There could not be any tigress — I argued with myself. Last day, I interviewed the General Manager also; he mentioned that even he had seen it on one night while he was returning from dinner at one friend's house. I asked him as to what were the tigress and its cubs doing when they were first seen. He said "they were sitting under a street light and the cubs were eating the insects (*Patangas*). Oh! No the tigress and its cubs feeding on insects cannot survive under any circumstances. Actually they also had seen a hyena with its cubs. Immediately after that I gave him in writing that there was no tiger in the area and there was nothing to be afraid of. They all were most probably seeing a hyena with cubs and were mistaking it for a tigress. We returned to Kanha and thereafter, there was never any complaint of a tiger in their mining area.

Episode-XV

The Man-eating Leopard of Kalegaon

During 1986-87 a leopard started attacking and lifting human beings in the bordering villages of Kanha National Park. It covered an area of about fifty sq. kms., between Kisli and Mukki. It had killed one and injured four persons. We tried to trap the animal in our drop shutter cages at various places, but all in vain. Mr. A.S. Parihar and I patrolled this area during night hours, many times, but there was no success. This animal became very daring. On one night, people had gathered at one place in village Jhuluk and they were chanting *'kirtan'*, this leopard dared to come near them. When they shouted at it, then only it ran away. That very night it entered the house of one *adivasi*, named Teeju Baiga at mid-night. These houses are generally *'kacha'* mud houses, without any doors in it. There is a small verandah in front, then a long room with an opening, but not a door. When needed, this opening is covered with a thin bamboo mat (a *chatai* or *tatta*). It acts more like a curtain than a door. The owner of the house and his wife were sleeping in this room only. The leopard came stealthily and caught hold of the man from his throat. It started dragging this man out of the house. On hearing his moan, the wife got up in the dark. By the time she could realize as to what was happening, the leopard had already gone about fifteen feet away with his catch, on the distal end of their verandah. She came running to the leopard and shouting at it, and started hitting the leopard with her wrists on its nape, as hard as she could. Actually, she had no time to search for any other weapon. All her glass bangles were broken, but she kept on hitting and shouting till this leopard left her husband and ran away. This brave woman could save her husband, with bare hands only, but had lost her speech temporarily for a few days. The husband had four puncture wounds in his neck and had to under go treatment for about a months time, but this brave man also survived.

Fig. 15.1: The Trap Cage with Staff and the Villagers of Kalegaon

Fig. 15.2: Mr. Venkatchellayya and Ms. Sharma with Villagers

Then this leopard killed a woman, Lasru Bai w/o Bhadu Baiga in village Kalegaon. The trap cage was put just in front of this house, with a dog as bait. On 18-6-87, I was on round of the park with Mr. Venkatchellayya, the justice from Supreme Court of India. The moment, we returned back to our Rest House at Kisli, I got a message that the leopard was trapped at Kalegaon, during last night, but the villagers were not letting out staff lift and bring the cage to Kanha. They were insisting on killing and burning the leopard there at that spot only. I was asked to come to the spot immediately. I asked our state guest, Mr. Venkatchellayya to excuse me as I had to rush to the spot. When we came to know about the incidence, even he wanted to come to the spot. I took him and Ms. Sharma, the then Registrar of Jabalpur High Court with me. When we reached village Kalegaon, we were shocked to see the mob of about five hundred persons, surrounding the cage. They were raising slogans, abusing the animal and were pocking rods in the cage in order to torture the animal. The leopard was agitated, it used to growl and then dash to the walls of the cage. The villagers had gathered a lot of dry grass, wood and hay to burn the animal.

When I requested them to leave the cage and let us take it to Kanha, they refused and were saying that we would again leave this animal in the forest, which would once again start killing their people. They wanted to kill and burn it there only. On seeing this, our justice Mr. Venkatchellayya sat under a tree and started chatting with them and asked me, what would I do now. Our Field Director, Mr. Lowalekar was staying at Mukki, about twenty kms. away. Even he was informed about it. He informed that he was also reaching the spot. People over there knew that he was also coming to Kalegaon. Then I told them not to take law in their hands and wait for him, he may agree with their demands. So they started waiting for him. We waited for half an hour but he did not turn up. People were getting restless. Another fifteen minutes wait, then I called my driver Raja Ram and told him in his ears to go straight to Baihar and get the police inspector with force, but in front of villagers said loudly "go to our Field Director, whose vehicle might have broken down and get him soon". The mob was satisfied that I had sent even my gypsy to fetch him soon, so they once again started waiting quietly. We waited for another one hour, then we saw the police inspector, Baihar coming on motor cycle with other force in my gypsy. On seeing police, all those self-made '*netas*' amongst villagers fled away and it did not take even five minutes to load our cage on the tractor trolley. Our justice said "Sharma, you have done it". Yes! I had done it luckily. In these villages, people are still afraid of police, therefore, any such operation, the police force is a must. Mr. Venkatchellayya was telling me that Sharma, if anything untowards happens here, justice from Supreme Court will stand witness to it. Luckily, that did not happen and we could rescue the animal from the clutches of enraged villagers.

1. **List of the persons injured by this leopard:**
   (i) Teeju s/o Manu Baiga, Jhulup.
   (ii) Hannu s/o Sohan Gond, Jhulup.
   (iii) Ganesh s/o Gorelal, Kumadehi.
   (iv) Phool Singh s/o Jhika Dhimar, Kashmiri – died later.

2. **List of the persons killed by this leopard:**
   (i) Lasru Bai w/o Bhadu Baiga, Kalegaon – killed and eaten.

Episode-XVI

Tiger in the Hut at Pandri-tikra

On Mandla-Raipur road, there is a small village Pandri-tikra, just on road side, a little beyond Bichhia. On the morning of 21-10-86, we received a message from D.F.O., East Mandla, that a tiger was sitting inside a house in this village and that the people were gathering around it. F.D.P.T., Kanha instructed me to reach the spot immediately along with Mr. M.P. Chacko, the Assistant Director. We packed up our equipment and the transportation cage and proceeded towards Pandri-tikra.

By the time we reached this village, it was around 2.00 p.m. The house concerned was hardly 200 mts. away from the main state highway. Almost 150-200 people had already gathered over there. People from Bichhia and other side were still coming by special transport, to see the tiger. The main mud house was on the southern side and a big '*Saar*' (room to keep the cattle in) was towards northern or the road side. There was about 12' wide open space between these two sections. The 'Saar' was having bamboo walls on three sides and the southern side was open with a railing of wooden poles. When we reached there, we were told that the tiger was sitting in this '*Saar*'. From one of the peepholes, we also saw that a tiger about two years of age was sitting near one of the vertical poles, which were supporting the tiled roof. It was facing towards road only, because it was listening human voices from that side, from where the people were peeping also at it. The peep holes were too small, that is why the tiger could not see the men looking at it, hence was not agitated or disturbed. Certainly, it was awake with its head lifted to listen. There was no man on the open side. Even the family members of the houseowner had come to northern side. It was again a strange thing, a tiger entering a house at day time, after the cattle had gone for grazing. It did not harm anybody.

We tried to find out a suitable opening, from where it could be tranquillized easily, but there was no other place than this bamboo wall. The tiger was sitting at

Fig. 16.1

Fig. 16.2

Fig. 16.3

about six to seven feet distance from it. It was all right to see the animal by sticking your eyes to the wall, but it was not possible to insert the barrel of the gun through it, lest it would have disturbed the animal. If we kept only the opening of the barrel in such a peep hole, we could only see the back and the foresight of the gun and not the object. So it was not possible to aim at the tiger. Again if we took a risk of shooting the dart on approximate aim, it could have hurt the animal in eyes or the face. It took about one hour, our darts were ready but our position was very odd. The crowd was growing bigger and bigger and we were losing time. It would have become further difficult, if it had moved away or to some other position. People in the crowd also start passing remarks and comments on your activities and make fun of you. At last we pushed the crowd a little away and I loaded the dart, took an approximate aim and fired. And when I peeped inside, I saw the dart on wooden pole, and not on the tiger, it just missed it. At such times, people are very curious and anxious of your results.

Now I did not want to take second chance from this position and waste my second dart also. Suddenly, I decided to take a risk, but a sure shot from the open railing side of the '*saar*'. Only myself and Mr. Chacko slowly walked to that open space, from here we had the full view of the tiger. To our good luck, it was still calm and looking in other direction, away from us. Without losing any further time, I aimed and fired the dart, which hit its rear thigh. The animal kept sitting there only. After about five minutes time, the head was down and we were in side the '*saar*' to lift this tiger. It was a small and very weak animal, perhaps was starving for some time. Maybe, it was sick also. After we brought it out, the villagers thronged upon us. After taking the measurements, etc. we put the animal in cage and brought it to Kanha. This animal did not survive for a long time and died in a month's time.

The reason again for straying of such a sub-adult tiger may be starving only and in search of food it started entering the village and houses. The forests this side might be having some cats but certainly, there is dearth of prey base.

Episode-XVII

The Man-killer of Saunf

In Kanha National Park, there is a meadow by name Saunf. It is actually a site of relocated village of Saunf. Right in the centre of the meadow, there flows a small nala, which retains water in the summer also. The grass is very tall in this meadow and, hence, it has become the main breeding ground for the Barasinga (the Swamp deer) of Kanha.

On 20-4-87 night, there broke a forest fire near this meadow. The forest guard and the five fire-watchers from Saunf camp, rushed immediately to the area and started control activity. It spread in a large area and they were busy almost whole night and then only it could be extinguished completely. It is a hilly area and once in 1979, Dr. P.C. Kotwal and I had to spend whole night here along with other staff to control such a fire. Anyway, when these fire-watchers were returning to Saunf camp, it was early morning about 5.00 a.m. There is a footpath that intersects this meadow of Saunf, and it directly leads to the Forest Guard *naka* and the camp for firewatchers. They were walking on this footpath, then one of them said "I am very thirsty, so I will go to the *nala* and better drink some water". He alone moved towards *nala* and others kept on moving towards the camp. Suddenly, they heard the loud roar of a tiger, which had charged and killed this firewatcher. From distance they could get a glimpse of tiger, who kept sitting near the dead body. But it was not eating it.

The message was flashed to Mandla H.Q. The Field Director and the then P.I.O., Mr. A.S. Parihar left for Saunf immediately. The elephants from Kanha were also ordered to reach the spot along with other equipments. By the time they reached Saunf, it was quite dark, the sun was setting, they could also see the tiger from a distance. It was too late to dart the tiger at this hour. Dr. Kotwal was on leave and I was busy with accounts, so Dr. Kotwal's assistant and these officers only decided to tranquillize this tiger. Since this tiger had already killed a man and was sitting near the dead body, they decided not to try it with the Tele-inject air gun (its range is short and it was dangerous to go very near this tiger on an elephant). So they decided to use a long range Dist-inject shot gun. But none of them had handled this weapon earlier. When they had a trial on dummy at the camp, it would not work. Well, from Mandla I sent a wireless message to inform me for any help or any equipment to be brought, as I was also to go to Kanha with Dr. Mandlekar, Veterinary Doctor for operation of one of the elephants. (Actually on reaching the site for tranquillization, one comes across many difficulties and sometimes you require certain things to complete the operation, such as wire, ropes, foam, medicines, etc.). But unfortunately the message sent by them could not reach me. So myself and Dr. Mandlekar left Mandla a bit leisurely, (we were to leave at 8.00 a.m., but left at 10.00 a.m.). First, we were going straight to Kanha via. Chiraidongri, but we changed our plan and went through Karibah gate, from Bichhia side, in order to know the result of operation tiger. When I reached Saunf camp, F.D.P.T. and P.I.O. were in the meadow. The Forest Guard told me "they were getting annoyed, as you are so late. They were waiting for you since morning, as they were not able to operate Dist-inject gun. I said, I did not get any message whatsoever. By chance, I have come to this side, due to my own curiosity and interest." Anyway, I joined the party on another elephant. It was around 12.30 p.m. and they had darted the animal once (by trial and error method, they learnt to use the gun). The tiger was a huge male, with a lot of injuries on its body. It was not down in ten minutes time. Actually, it was quite agitated and furious. Then a second dart was given and it was down in another ten minutes time. This was a local resident tiger of Sandukhol area of Kisli, which had a severe fight with another large male tiger of Kanha ghat, two days back. This tiger lost its territory and migrated to Saunf with its injuries and just to ward off flies, was hiding in tall grass near that *nala*. As this fire-watcher reached suddenly, this tiger already in a bad mood, felt offensive and charged. Subsequently, killed him. It was not a man-eater. It kept sitting near the dead body for whole night, but did not eat any part of it.

The tiger was put in a squeeze cage, which was already kept on a tractor trolley. Actually our transportation cage was busy elsewhere on that day, in other such operation. Instructions were given to the Range Assistant, Mr. Bisen to unload the cage at Kanha and be kept in *Deshi nala*, slightly tilted in such a way that a corner is submerged and tiger could drink water as soon as it came back into its senses. After some time, when I reached Kanha and asked about the whereabouts of the tiger cage, I was taken to a spot 1.5 kms. away from Kanha on link road number nine. I was astonished to find that the cage was unloaded on a raised hillock type of place. The tiger was fully awake and very furious. On seeing human beings approaching, used to roar and shake the entire cage badly, by dashing against the sidewalls. When I asked him as to what had he done, he said he could not follow the instructions. The instructions were clear but his intentions were not. So the tiger was furious and it could not be given any water in such conditions. Those who have taken part in such operations know that these animals need a lot of water after tranquillization, in order to excrete the drug through urination.

I came back to my camp to wait for the tiger to calm down and also for the operation on the wound of our elephant. At about 5.00 p.m., Mr. Lowalekar, F.D.P.T., Mr. Parihar, P.I.O. and Mr. Bittu Sehgal, the Editor of *Sanctuary* magazine came from Kisli and wanted to see the tiger. I told them all about its condition. I told them that the shutter of the cage was also not locked and if by chance the tiger gave it a big jerk, it may topple opening its door also. And if this tiger came out of cage, may become a problem again. So they also dropped the idea of disturbing it once again.

In the night around 1.30 a.m., there was a knock at my door. It was Mr. Parihar, who was staying at Kisli. I was a bit shocked to see him at this mid-night. When I asked him the reason, he said in a nervous tone, *"Sharma sahib jaldi kapade badlo, bahut gadbad ho gaya hai"* (Mr. Sharma, hurry up, change your clothes, something serious has gone wrong). I was also little worried now and asked him again the reason of his visit. He said "your tiger has come out of the cage, before it harms anybody we have to do something". I could not believe it, because I staying there at Kanha only, could not know this and he was knowing. Then the way he was acting, I had to give in and went to the dressing room for changing my clothes. When I returned, I saw Mr. Parihar sleeping calmly on the other bed of my room. Now I was sure that it was not true, otherwise one cannot sleep comfortably in such a condition. I now woke him up and asked him the truth. Then he said *"Nahin Sharmaji, woh garib sher pyasa hoga, chalo usko pani pilayenge"* (Mr. Sharma, that poor tiger must be thirsty, let us go and give him some water). Yes! I agreed to it and myself, Mr. Parihar, driver Rajaram, waiter Hiran and Mr. Bisen R.A., Kanha left for the spot again. We had a bucket full of water, a small rubber pipe with us. Our plan was to approach the cage from rear side very slowly, without disturbing the tiger, keep bucket on the top of the cage, then siphon the water with the help of rubber pipe and drop it into the cage. The tiger will lick it slowly and take maximum of it, that it could take in this fashion.

We left our vehicle at about 100 mts. away and started moving towards the cage in the darkness of the night. On our side, there were many trees and quite shady, we were moving without talking to each other. When we were very near the cage, our tiger woke up and could sense our approach but could not clearly make out a human approach. It growled very slowly. Hiran was holding the bucket which was later kept on the cage, as slowly as possible. Then Rajaram sucked water and it started flowing into the cage. The tiger was really very thirsty and immediately started lapping it. After a minute or two, suddenly sensing us so near its cage, the tiger gave a deafening roar showing its utter intolerance to human beings. Our waiter Hiran was terrified and left the bucket, which toppled, on the cage and the water fell inside the cage. Rajaram shouted at him *"Saale.... hai to aise kaam ke liye kyon chale aate ho"* (if you are so afraid why do you come for such jobs). Anyway, our drama was over. We were happy that it had some water at least. Mr. Parihar left for Kisli and myslf for my room.

Next day, Mr. Lowalekar, Mr. Parihar and Mr. Bittu Sehgal left for Supkhar, direct from Kisli via Mukki. I hurriedly finished with my breakfast and again came to our tiger. It was fully agile and was again charging at any human approach. I took some time to decide my course of action and what method to adopt to tranquillize it again and transport it to our permanent cages at Kanha. At last I decided to use blowgun for the first time in real operation. I prepared two darts as usual and started moving slowly on my knees towards the cage. I put a few persons on other side at a distance, to attract the tiger and divert its attention from me. It worked very well and and after crawling for fifteen minutes, I was at the cage unnoticed. It was darted easily and was down in five minutes time. Although our tractor and trolley was ready, it could not reach just next to the cage. Our squeeze cage was very heavy and about 10-15 persons were required to lift it at the trolley height. The freshly cut poles were slipping under the iron cage and our team of ten persons was not able to move the cage. More persons were called, and then with great difficulty the cage was brought near the trolley. We had already lost about half an hour's time since it was down. I was not willing to give it additional dose of drug.

Again I shouted at them to hurry up. Another ten minutes, it was on the trolley and we moved it to Kanha. Our permanent cage had two drop-shutters. Both of these shutters were kept open in advance, was cleaned properly and water was ready in the small water tanks inside the cage. Two big bamboo mats were ready to cover the shutters from outside, so that tiger could not see the human beings coming or moving near the cage. At this permanent cage, when I opened the shutter of our squeeze cage to lift the tiger and transfer it, it was about fifty five minutes past since it was down. We hurried up and four persons lifted and started moving towards the permanent cage. Two persons from the head side entered in, they rushed out from the distal shutter after keeping the tiger down. I got the shutter closed immediately. Then I asked these two persons, who were on the rear side and still in side the cage, to retreat through the shutter of their entry. The reason was that our tiger had started moving its ears by this time. Immediately this shutter was also dropped, and locked. Bamboo mats were erected on both the openings. And lo! I could clearly hear our tiger inside lapping water. It was up and was very thirsty. We were just in time to finish our job. Late by a couple of minutes could have been dangerous. I thanked my stars and walked slowly to my lower cabin.

This time we learnt that a job should never be left to the lower functionaries alone. Anytime they can put you in such a situation. Sometimes, they cannot think beyond a certain level and sometimes they just misunderstand. Once a lord of Kisli jungle, killed a man accidentally, and then put in jail on 22-4-87. This tiger ultimately died on 12-6-87, due to paralysis.

Episode-XVIII

The Rabid Tigress of Khitauli

In the year 1981-82, when I was posted in Bandhavgarh National Park, one night I received a message at my residence at Umaria that a full grown tigress had been locked in timber depot hut at Khitauli. It had a quill of porcupine on her right paw, which was taken out by my Assistant Director, Mr. G. D. Dwivedi. I thought there was no point in going in the middle of the night as it was already locked inside the hut.

As the story was told to me, one coupe guard of regular division of Jabalpur [Khitauli is the H.Q. of a Range of Jabalpur (now Katni) division, on the border of Bandhavgarh National Park] was returning from the coupe after days work. It was evening time and he was accompanied by a labourer. The coupe was located on Khitauli-Umaria road, just outside the park. When they reached a stream to have a wash near forest village Bagdari, they saw a tigress sitting in the water. From a distance, it appeared to be a full-grown tigress. Seeing a tiger in these forests was not a rare thing for them. From behind a tree, they shouted at it. Surprisingly, it did not show much of reaction. Now they gathered courage and started pelting stones at it. On this, she got up, looked at them, a cool stare and came out of water. It did never charge at them and it was standing with its head down. This great guard and his companion gathered more courage and went near it further. And now it was not a tigress for them, but a 'cow'. With the help of a stick they started herding and directing the tigress towards Khitauli, which was around four kilometres away. And one won't believe it, these two chaps brought this tigress to Khitauli. Just on the entrance of the village was a small timber depot, with a small hut made of bamboos and mud. They asked everybody to come out and made this tigress enter it. Then they put the door on (made of bamboo mat) and informed immediately to my Assistant Director at Tala. By about 8.30 p.m., he reached Khitauli and saw the tigress. It was having a porcupine quill in her one foot. He put his hand slowly and pulled it out. It appeared weak and starving, perhaps other smaller quills were stuck in its throat. The then Range Officer Khitauli, Mr. Makin had put some milk in a pan to feed her but it did not touch it.

Next morning I came early to the Government Veterinary Doctor, Umaria, and one Panditji from Rewa. Asked him to accompany me and treat the tigress suitably. He was reluctant to come for the tigress. I encouraged him and somehow made him to come with me. But what to carry and what not, was not clear to him. I asked him to carry the biggest syringe and a lot of injectable glucose. I said, "it appears to be starving and very weak, by injecting glucose we may be able to give some strength to it. At the same time I had sent a message to Kanha National Park also to send a party and cage, so that it could be shifted to Veterinary College Jabalpur, for treatment. That time, there were no such facilities available at Bandhavgarh. So, when Veterinary Doctor and I reached at about 9.30 a.m., we saw that the tigress was sleeping inside. From little opening on top of the bamboo shutter (*khatka*), it was hardly five feet away. I shouted at it, knocked at the shutter but she was having no reaction. Before our arrival the Range Officer had left a small live lamb inside, just to feed her, but she was not interested in it also. The lamb was freely moving and jumping inside, from this corner to the other but our tigress was unmoved. It did not open its eyes even. It was breathing slowly and sleeping constantly. Now I gathered courage and entered the hut after removing shutter, clapped near her and asked the 'queen' as to what was wrong with her, no reaction or no answer. I called Doctor to come and examine it, but he refused even to enter the hut. Then I asked him if the glucose could be injected through tail also. He said "yes! it will be slow in absorption, but we can do it". I came out, put the shutter back on. The tigress was lying just adjacent to the side wall. I got a small opening made on the wall near her tail and took it out. Asked four persons to hold the tail and then Doctor to inject glucose. I came to the shutter and from the opening started observing the animal and its reaction. First, the tigress got up, sat lifting its head and fore-legs only. Still it was sitting on its hind legs and our team was still injecting glucose, with its tail out. After two minutes suddenly it started struggling to be free, also it started looking at the lamb which was running here and there, due to fear. The tigress was trying to take a leap on the lamb. Then I thought it better to leave. I was thinking that she was gaining strength and normal behaviour and due such jerk may become normal. So I ordered them to leave its tail. She immediately pounced upon the lamb, caught hold of its neck and sat. But then no further movement. A strange thing. She kept on sitting like this only for a long time, the lamb was dead but she did not eat it. Again she went to sleep at a different position now. The Doctor was so much scared, he said, "had I come in and injected the glucose inside the hut, even I would have got the same fate, as that of the lamb". Then we came back to Umaria, to wait further for the Kanha team.

The Kanha team with Mr. A.S. Parihar, the then Deputy Director and Dr. P.C. Kotwal, Research Officer reached Umaria at about 8.30 p.m. We had hurried dinner and then proceeded once again for Khitauli. By the time we arrived here, it was

12.30 a.m. When we peeped inside, our tigress was moving briskly, from one comer to the other. Apparently it looked very normal, except that it had gone weak and had not fed for many days. We decided not to tranquillize this weak animal and instead of that make her to walk into our transportation cage directly (a blind cage). We put the cage at the place of bamboo shutter, and with a lot of persuasion, ultimately she walked in. It was around 5.00 a.m., when the cage was loaded on our van. Mr. Parihar decided to go straight to the Veterinary college at Jabalpur and not waste anytime further. So they left immediately for Jabalpur.

There at Veterinary College, Jabalpur also the Doctors were a little afraid to handle the tigress. They were a bit worried about the Wildlife Act and its provisions. They delayed action further for two days. When Mr. H.S. Panwar, the then Field Director, Kanha returned from Delhi on third day and shouted at them, they agreed to treat the animal. By now, the tigress had become more weak and harmless. The men could handle it with bare hands. Not one or two but then four Doctors started investigations and treatment. But they were too late and she died on that day.

Later on its brain was perhaps sent to Dr. Hiresh Chandra for Forensic studies. After some days, I received a letter from him asking me to investigate in the field, if any village dogs also died during that period with same symptoms, as the tigress had. According to him it was a dumb type of 'Rabies', in which the animal becomes very docile. Our enquiries showed no such cases, but she died with these symptoms. If rabid, she had to die in any case, but dying without or late medical attendance was unfortunate. Even timely and the 'brave' act of that coupe guard and the labour could not save her.

Episode-XIX

The Ego Clash between the Park and District Administration

All these years, I have seen one more particular thing in day-to-day administration, which I would like to mention here. With the National Parks and wildlife getting more and more attention of public, the park officials also started getting more fame and attention. At the district level, it is not palatable to other officers of various departments, especially revenue. Most of the Collectors and S.Ps. do not like park officials getting importance. (Exceptions are always there and I know certain I.A.S. and I.P.S. officers who gave full support and always gave due respect to the park officers too). This type of indigestion, sometimes, becomes very dangerous.

Kanha has a different position. Every V.V.I.P. like President, Prime Minister, Chief Ministers, all high level committees, etc. are visiting Kanha, there by, the Field Director and other staff are coming in direct contact with them, hence, they command a special position at the district level. Although the collector and other departmental heads are most of the time busy showing Kanha National Park to the V.V.I.Ps., their bosses, family members and friends, so they do talk sweetly and respectfully to Kanha officials. But certainly they are always in search of such opportunities, when they can have an upper hand and snub them.

Generally, they expect that persons from their side should be treated as V.I.Ps. and all facilities be provided to them free of cost and the Director should attend to them in the park also. It is very unfortunate. All should know that now in parks like Kanha, Bandhavgarh, Panna, Shivpuri and Pench, thousands of tourists are coming every year. And hundreds of them are of V.V.I.P, V.I.P status, whom the Director has to attend compulsorily. Then he has to attend his day-to-day other works of the park also, he is not only a receptionist of a hotel or tourist spot. The pressure on Forest Rest Houses inside the park is also tremendous. Everybody wants to stay in these only.

Once all of the rooms are booked, it can't be cancelled and given to others, how-soever important person he is. But P.As. of Ministers, secretaries, commissioners and collectors just send a requisition and want it in any case. It is single sided communication, nobody likes to know whether any accommodation is available on that particular day or not. They only say that such and such person is reaching on such and such day and that is all. The district collectors want to have full control on the Forest Rest Houses, situated inside the National Parks also, as they are having on the circuit houses of P.W.D. But any such action will jeopardize the very cause of wildlife conservation. These Rest Houses are housing V.V.I.Ps., wildlife experts, various wildlife functionaries from centre, other states and abroad and the collectors interference will be great hindrance. Secondly, these are Forest Rest Houses and the first right to stay in is that of a Forest Officer on duty or tour and anybody's booking can be cancelled in his favour.

Once in 1979, some Bidi Patta Wala Patel from Jabalpur sent a requisition (verbal), that also through C.F. Jabalpur for reservation of Kisli F.R.H. for seven days and all of the six suites. Since they were vacant, were booked in his name. After two days, suddenly an express message came from Delhi that seven Chief Wildlife Wardens from various states were coming to Kanha for three days, covering the first three days of the same dates. We had no other option than to cancel the booking of that Bidiwala Patel for first three days, retaining the reservation of the later four days. Immediately it was informed to them also. But this Bidiwala company did not turn up at all. Instead, after a few days a complaint was lodged by them to the then Forest Secretary, that they had some foreigner guests, to whom they wanted to show Kanha and that due to this cancellation could not visit. They alleged that it was wrong to have cancelled reservation in favour of 'so-called V.I.Ps'. Towards explanation I had to say that before getting a Forest Rest House reserved, one must know that it can be cancelled in favour of any Forest Officer visiting on the same dates. Secondly, we retained their reservation for the remaining four days, which was sufficient duration to show Kanha, had they really wanted to show to their 'so-called foreigner guests'. Our Chief Wildlife Wardens were not so-called V.I.Ps, but were in real sense V.I.Ps for us and got preference on anybody else.

Once in 1985 at Kanha, the ego clash in booking F.R.H., Kisli took an ugly turn. Our Prime Minister, late Shri Rajeev Gandhi was to visit Kanha during Holi and it was a private visit of the family members. The then Collector Mandla, one Mr. Singhai wanted to book the Kisli F.R.H. at his level. Our Field Director refused this and told him that it was our priviledge. And on the contrary, collector should send the names of the officers, in whose favour he wanted bookings. He told him that we would take due care and book the rooms as per protocol, so he needed not to worry on this accord. Two days prior to P.M's. visit, this collector came to Kanha and Kisli to see the preparations. There at Kisli, when he saw the reservation slips at the F.R.H., he lost his temper. His false ego was hurt and started shouting as to who had done these reservations. All the staff was busy elsewhere, only room attendant was there, he said that his F.D.P.T. had done so. Collector said "No, I have already booked in my office, how can he do it" then he asked him to open the rooms, the attendant refused saying that it would be opened only when these officers come to stay here, otherwise room setting will be disturbed, if opened every now and then. The Collector asked about the keys and as soon as he showed him the keys, collector snatched it and kept in his pocket. The attendant requested him to return the keys, but he did not and moved on his way to Mandla in his vehicle.

Immediately, the matter was informed to our Field Director at Mandla, who in turn ordered to request the Collector to return the keys, if he was still in the park and if he did not return, the keys may be snatched from him. The Collector was still in the park. Our Range Assistant, Kisli, immediately rushed to Khatia gate and got it locked. As the vehicle of Collector reached Khatia on way to Mandla, it was stopped. R.A. asked him to return the keys of our F.R.H. The Collector threatened him that he was talking to the Collector. The R.A., Mr. Basta Ram Nagpure said, "Yes! I know, but I have to obey my F.D.P.T., you can deal with him at your level but you cannot take the keys from here. The gate will be opened only when you return the keys. Ultimately, the Collector had to return the keys, before going to Mandla. But this incident became one of the causes for making a complaint against F.D.P.T. after the visit of the P.M.

Mr. Lowalekar, our F.D.P.T. talked immediately to the then Commissioner, Jabalpur and expressed his inability to welcome the P.M. under such circumstances, who in turn asked him to continue the preparations and also that these youngsters are like that only, so he needed not to worry. He also assured that he would look in to the matter after P.M.'s visit. On his assurance, we kept on working hard for the P.M.'s stay at Kanha. He stayed in Kanha with his family for three days and every thing went well. Hardly ten minutes after his helicopter left, the Commissioner while leaving for Jabalpur, stopped for a while and instructed the Collector, saying "Don't forget we have to send the complaint". And after a weeks time our F.D.P.T. received a letter from Government of M.P., calling for his explanation on complaint by the Collector, Mandla. It said that the arrangements during the P.M.'s visit were inadequate and the F.D.P.T. did not co-operate with the district administration. We were happy that visit of P.M. went well, because three days stay of a V.V.I.P. with all family members, personal physician, personal security (about 50 commandos) at a place like Kanha and absolutely no lapse of any kind. On the top of it, the P.M. did not allow anybody inside park except park officials, not even Collector or S.P. This type of arrangements were not being tolerated by these officers. They were so much jealous that on last day, when P.M. permitted the families of park officials to come to Kanha to meet him, their vehicle was not being permitted to enter at Khatia Gate by S.P. himself. He was sitting at Khatia Gate and was not believing it and detained the vehicle at least for half an hour. Ultimately, instructions were issued directly from P.M.'s Rest House again and then only he allowed the vehicle to enter.

A lot of panic was there on receiving this letter from the Government and any normal officer would have knelt down under pressure, but the person in Mr. Lowalekar never knew this. Due to his virtues and skills, he replied this letter of eleven lines in a big volume of 105 pages (later on condensed into 55 pages). It contained a befitting reply. An authority, who was not permitted inside the park during entire period of stay, was commenting on inadequacy. The P.M. himself had written in his comments that the arrangements were excellent and all praise for park officials and the staff. It was really an unfortunate situation, created due to immature thinking, jealousy and ego problem. Anyhow, the Collector was immediately shifted from Mandla and nothing untowards happened to the park officials. The successor collector was cautious from the beginning only. In the first week of his joining, he wrote a D.O. letter to our F.D.P.T., requesting for a new set of arrangements regarding booking of Rest House, round of the park by the official visitors, their food and all. Once again a clear-cut reply was given to him, explaining that our R.H. is always booked as per protocol, at the very moment a requisition is sent by the collector, the vehicles of our park officials in which certain visitors are taken around are not tourist vehicles, but vehicles allotted to these officers for their own tours and inspections of works, so expecting availability of these vehicles all the time is wrong. Then catering is not the job of park officials. One should make his own arrangements through M.P. tourism units, which are established for this purpose only. These things should be very clear in the minds of all officers at district and state capital level.

In another incident, which took place at Bandhavgarh in 1981, the things were a little different. Our F.R.H., Tala was having only four suites and all used to be given to the tourists on demand and advance payment of rent in full. When I joined in April 1980, I felt that it was wrong to give all the rooms to tourists, because a sudden arrival of any senior Forest Officer put us in trouble. It was not possible to cancel any booking of tourist after accepting rent in advance. So on my own, I started retaining one suite un-allotted, which could be given to the government officers on demand. The then collector, Shahdol, Mr. R.K. Sahni was till then a good friend of mine. During the month of March, Commissioner, Rewa made a programme of coming to Bandhavgarh. On getting information, I reserved suite no. 1 available with me for the commissioner. The remaining three suites were already booked by some Gujarati families of Katni. A day before his arrival, I had to go to Jabalpur and book the remaining budget, that being the year ending month. So after making the necessary arrangements and deputing my Assistant Director for the job, I came to Jabalpur expecting to return by night. Somehow, I could not return, before the departure of the commissioner. Although his visit was comfortable and O.K., still the collector went unhappy, because he could not get a room in the F.R.H. As told by the Assistant Director, on his arrival at Tala, he asked about his room. He was told that the remaining three suites were occupied by the tourists, so he had to stay in White Tiger Lodge of M.P. Tourism Development Corporation or the P.W.D. Rest House. He did not like it and asked about me. He was told that I had gone to Jabalpur for some urgent work and would return in the night if work is completed. Anyway, next day, I got a call from collector, who said that he was not happy during his last visit. The obvious reason was room allotment. He asked me four questions: (1) why so many suites were given to tourists, (2) why were they given for five days at a stretch, (3) why 3-4 persons were staying in each room of double bed only, and (4) why could I not cancel their reservation on knowing about the visit of collector and commissioner. I told him that till then there existed no such guidelines regarding room reservations and even this one suite given to the commissioner was retained by me on my own. He said, "then get the guide lines from your head office". Next day, I wrote to my Chief Wildlife Warden and sought clear instructions on this, so that there was no further confusion on such issues. The reply I got was: (1) Only two suites out of four, may be given to the tourists, (2) Maximum for three nights, it could be given to one party at a stretch, (3) Any number of persons could stay in a room, if they could adjust them selves, and (4) No authority including collector could cancel the reservation of a tourist at any cost.

It was enough for me. Some more time passed and the commissioner (Mr. Bhatnagar) visited once again and I attended his trip personally this time. He was very happy and was keen to know the procedure of counting the animals. He wanted to join our census work in our park. So I sent him the dates, on which we were counting our animals. S.D.O., police, Umaria informed me on phone regarding dates of arrival of D.I.G., Rewa and commissioner, Rewa and requested reservation for two suites only for them. It was done, then came some tourists from Katni and wanted two rooms and got it done as per rules. At about 5.00 p.m., I got a phone from S.D.M., Umaria, asking for all the four suites, for their visit, saying that Collector and S.P. from Shahdol would also come and stay. I told him that I was sorry, as other two rooms were got reserved by some tourist party and they had already gone to stay there. After some time, again he called me and said that collector wanted me to cancel the reservation of tourists. I expressed my inability to do so and told him that they could stay in White Tiger Lodge or the P.W.D. Rest House easily.

I did not have a telephone at my residence. At about 6.30 p.m., I was informed that there was a call from collector, Shahdol at Tahsildar's residence and that he was waiting for me on line. When I picked up and wished him, he said, "*Sharmaji aajkal aap kuchh jyada niyam bata rahe hain*" (Mr. Sharma, you are observing many rules these days). I asked him as to which rules he was talking about and if it was regarding reservation of rest house, then I was sorry, as I could not help it. He asked me to cancel the booking of the tourists staying over there. I told him that it was not possible. Again he asserted saying "I am saying it, you cancel it". Then I told him that our Chief had already issued guidelines on this and no authority could cancel a tourist's reservation once confirmed. He was annoyed on this and then said "send me a copy of that, I will deal with it". I told him that why was he getting annoyed unnecessarily, if I had the rooms, why would I annoy a collector.

At the time Dy. S.P., Umaria asked for only two rooms, all were vacant and had he informed about your arrival also, I would have given all the four. After half an hour, the tourists came and booked remaining two rooms, then how can I help now. All rooms in P.W.D. Rest House and the white tiger lodge are vacant and they could stay there easily, what was the problem. He told, "*Sharma sahib soch lijiye*" (Mr. Sharma, think over it). On this I said "*is mein sochane ka kya hai*" (what is there to think on it). Again he said in a threatening tone "*soch lijiye*" (think about it). My reply was "*Hamne jo sochana tha soch liya, ab aap hi soch lijiye*" (I have thought, now you may think as you like). On this he said, "you are talking irrelevant". I said, you started it, why are you threatening. Then he said, "*Mr. Sharma, phone par baat ho rahi hai, saamne hote to dekh leta*" (Mr. Sharma, we are talking on phone, had you been in front of me, I would have seen you). It was limit, then was my reply, "*sahib, kal aap Tala mein aayenge, wahin dekh lena*" (Sir, tomorrow you are coming to Tala, you may see me there only) and I kept the phone down.

Next day in the evening, I was waiting for the party to arrive, in front of our rest house. The Collector and S.P. came there, I wished them. S.P. replied but not the collector, he started facing other side, S.P. sat on the next chair and the collector on further next. Suddenly the car of tourists was parked in front of their suites. S.P. asked as to what was the matter. I told him that they have seen the park and the tigers, now they are leaving back home prematurely. Why? He asked. I told them that our staff had informed them that next day no vehicle was being allowed in, due to census work. So they thought that there was no point in staying back. S.P. asked me, if that was true, I said "No, census will be carried out up to 9.00 a.m. and all tourist vehicles will be allowed in only after 9.00 a.m., if they (tourists) asked me, I would tell them the correct position. Then for the first time collector opened his mouth and told me to keep sitting there only. Soon both those suites were also vacant; I got them also set and ready. S.P. and Collector were at ease now.

After some time, when commissioner's party arrived in four vehicles, over flowing with persons, the Collector commented, "Oh! they are also coming like those Gujarati tourists". Then I told him that all come like this only, with families and friends, to enjoy the nature. The Commissioner, Collector, D.I.G. and S.P., Rewa were there with families, children, *ayas*, sentries, etc. The Commissioner on first look came rushing to me, shook hands and then asked as to what was there to be shown that evening and all. Soon, we were there, ready for the evening round, our collector mischievously made all the females sit in my jeep to lead and I was to drive them. In next jeep, the collector to drive and all males to sit in that jeep to follow us. Our collector knew that the wife and the daughter of our commissioner were keen wildlifers and used to stop at each chital even and would not let you move till they explained each body part of it and praised it in full. Anyway after a fruitful trip of two hours, in which we could see all animals, including tigers on the road, gaurs, bears, chitals, sambars and hyenas, we returned to F.R.H. And now this collector in good mood said, "Sharma sahib, salute to your stamina that you could withstand all of them for so long (indicating towards ladies)". Actually our collector was a bachelor till then.

All thrilled visitors were taken to the forest for morning and evening rounds on next day also, shown many wildlife films during night and even during after noon after lunch. They were all fully satisfied, so also my collector. After they left next evening, our collector shook hands and thanked me for everything and said that he never expected it to be like this. I said "it was my duty and we are professionals in our job and we do see that all go satisfied from here. This short lived bitterness was there between us and was surely due to ego problem. But still I praise this collector of mine, who afterwards, never talked about it and never showed any annoyance. One good thing in him was that he always talked himself on phone. He never asked his steno or Dy. Collector to talk on his behalf, who generally misguide them on smallest issues.

One such case happened in 1997. On First January, all the four suites were booked by our local M.L.A., as his relative was to come from Delhi (also an M.P. and ex-minister at centre). I was also at Tala on that day. When I came back to Umaria, I was told by my steno that S.D.M., Umaria wanted one room for the then Collector and that the actual position was told to the S.D.M. On this, the S.D.M. said that it would be all right if the collector is allowed to use the Director's camp residence. My steno said O.K. and assured him to inform me accordingly. I said O.K., but the time of his arrival was not informed by anybody. It was first day of the month, I was holding the monthly meeting in my office, where my Assistant Director and all Range Officers were present. Suddenly at 11.30 a.m., we got a wireless message from Tala, that Collector was there. He was very furious and was asking about his room. The Range Assistant was instructed to take him to the Field Director's cabin, but he refused to go. Till then there was no revenue staff also over there, evidently even they were unaware of his programme. He kept on insisting for suite No.1 only. By that time, our M.L.A. was also back from the Bandhavgarh fort and when he knew the situation, he agreed to vacate any room than suite No.1., where his guest was staying. I immediately sent my Assistant Director and Range Officer back to Tala and sort out things. The S.D.M. also reached, but the collector was not ready to listen to anybody. He did not accept even a glass of water served to him. He kept on shouting on the S.D.M. and our staff and asked S.D.M. to check all our muster rolls. Then he left back to Shahdol. What was that? Only ego problem? Had he the courtesy of calling me directly and knowing the exact position, could have postponed his visit by one day more. From Shahdol, he could have come any time again. This S.D.M. never informed him back the exact position and thought on his own that the collector will happily stay in Field Director's cabin. Anyway, such mishaps can be easily avoided if collectors and other district officers shed their ego, understand the working of the parks and co-operate with already overburdened park officials.

Episode-XX

Some Episodes of Baiting Activities in the Parks

When I joined in Kanha Tiger Reserve in 1978, luring and localizing tigers by giving baits was quite common. In Kanha, this activity increased, when Mr. George. B. Schaller worked here in early 70s. That time we used to bait our tigers with small buffalo calves, at least once a week. It was prevalent in Kanha and Bandhavgarh both. The villagers around these parks after knowing that these buffalo calves purchased by us were being fed to the tigers, stopped selling their calves to us. Then we started getting these from Nagpur by truck loads. Even the tourists could get it tied, after paying the cost of a buffalo calf, the bait, on anyday of the week. The baiting used to be done for maximum one or two tigers in Kanha/Kisli/Mukki and not the entire population of tigers. There used to be a lot of controversy on baiting activity in Kanha, lest it would change the habits of tigers, etc. But I know of certain that it was not the least detrimental to the tigers, no tiger ever became erratic due to baiting. On the contrary, it helped in showing the tigers closely to the tourists, who enjoyed and photographed tigers and our parks and the wildlife got a lot of publicity. But subsequently, during a visit of our late Prime Minister Mrs. Indira Gandhi to Gir National Park in Gujarat in 1982, a live pig was given as a bait to the lions. These lions started eating the bait without killing it. It was a very pathetic scene and she was moved so much that she asked as to where else these baits were being given to the Tigers/Lions. When she came to know that this activity was going on in most of the National Parks of the country, she passed an order to stop baiting in all the parks, with immediate effect. Since then no baits are being given to the tigers in these parks.

Some interesting stories about baits are as follows:

1. Once in 1979, I was staying at Kanha. In the morning our Range Officer, Mr. M.P. Chacko informed me that one of the baits in the stock room died in the night and he threw its dead body near link road No. 9. Also that a tiger had come and started eating it. I was shocked to know it. I told him that the dead body should have been shown to our Veterinary Doctor, to ensure that it had not died of dome infectious disease, which in turn would have infected our wild animals also. So we decided to get the post mortem done now. We called our Veterinary Doctor from Kisli (Dr. Chaudhary) and immediately rushed to the spot on elephants. We made the tiger move away, who had just started opening the carcass. Then we got down to it. Our great Manglu Baiga of Kanha, who had actually opened a number of wild animals for post mortem on several occasions, was not willing to touch it. When I asked for the reason, he replied that he was *adivasi* Baiga and not a "*chamaar*", he could open a wild animal, but not cattle. It was the job of a *chamaar*. On my insisting, he agreed for it as a government duty, but then started asking Bansi Baiga to assist him, who also was reluctant to touch it. Luckily, there was no disease found in it. But even then I got it buried in the ground. After that when Manglu was taking a wash on nearby *nala*, he started grinning and said "there is no worry now, because the only other villager over there was Bansi, who had also touched the dead body of our bait and assisted in post mortem. Now, he will not complain against him to their village people."
2. There at Bandhavgarh, we had an elephant by name Kalyani or Kallu and its mahaut by name Laphantu. Both of them belonged to one time famous circus, the "Kamla circus". The others, almost all members of the circus drowned in the sea while returning from some South-East country. Hence, the owner had donated the elephant with the mahaut to the Forest Department of M.P. Kallu used to break coconut on Lord Shiva, i.e. *Shivalinga* in the circus, pour water on it and then garland it. Here in Bandhavgarh also, just out of old memory, sometimes it used to spray water on the tiger also. Mostly, the tigers on getting these showers, changed their position, but at times were giving a big roar also. The mahaut Laphantu also became eccentric due to death of his people and circus mates. Mostly he used to remain alone. He was single and at times used to cry in hysterical fits remembering his friends and colleagues. On every pay day, he used to sit at the small hotel at Tala and offer sweets, tea, etc. from his own pocket to every passenger of bus or people coming to the hotel. By evening, used to spend whole of his pay and come back to his quarter. He had nothing in his house, so never used to lock his room. Whole month then he used to beg food from his colleague mahauts/ *chara*-cutters. That was his lifestyle.

One day, Mr. Tom Nebbia, the staff photographer of National Geographic came to Bandhavgarh from Kanha. He was preparing a photographic story of tiger and during one weeks stay, could not get much sequence in Kanha. So Mr. H.S. Panwar, the then Director of Kanha asked him to go to Bandhavgarh. At that time, Bandhavgarh was not known to media and people abroad. Therefore, with great reluctance he came to Bandhavgarh. And just on arrival, he was taken to Jamunia site, where a tiger was being shown, sitting in water. Mr. Tom Nebbia said to me "this is a piece of cake for me". I said "you will get a lot of bread and butter also, so do not worry". That was the time, when I could show a tigress with four cubs in Chorbahra *nala* at anytime of the day. She was so much localized in that area due to continuous baiting that it hardly went away from it. So Mr. Nebbia started having photo sessions with this family also and was very happy and satisfied. After about ten days, I asked him that when was he going back to Kanha. He said "no! I am not going to Kanha, this is heaven for me".

A day before 'Holi', I came to him to inform him that I was leaving for my H.Q. at Umaria for the festival and in my absence my Range Officer, Mr. Ashutosh Dubey would be looking after his programme. And then I could not go back to Tala, due to other exigencies. He was there at Tala for about twenty days and went back to U.S.A., straight from there only. On his way back, from Delhi he rang up to Mr. J.J. Dutta, our C.W.L.W. at Bhopal. He was complaining that his stay at Tala was excellent till Mr. Sharma was there at Tala. After his departure, he had very tough time and that a written complaint was being sent to him. At that moment, I was sitting in front of Mr. Dutta, in his chamber. When he asked me about it, I did not know anything, actually when I left him at Tala, he was very happy and fully satisfied. At that very moment, we received the written complaint also by post. I got a copy that was all against my R.O. Dubey and this Laphantu mahaut. Mr. Dubey was a drunkard, who used to remain awake till very late in the night and then sleep till very late in the morning or even noon sometimes. Except this big drawback, he was a fine person. During my enquiry it came into light that due to this bad habit, even after promising Mr. Nebbia to meet in the morning to accompany him for certain shoots, this fellow did not turn up and kept on sleeping on most of the occasions. One day he got bait tied for the tigress and four cubs at Chorbahra for a photo sequence. When Mr. Nebbia reached the site in the morning, there was no bait/no tigress. Later on he came to know that some mahaut untied the bait and took it away. Mr. Nebbia took it as a sabotage of his programme, which might have been managed by Mr. Dubey, R.O. only. On detailed enquiry, it was found that the bait was untied by none else than Mr. Laphantu mahaut. On lot of persuasion also, he did not name any body else for this act. He said that he had reached the site, before all other elephants, the bait was not killed and the rope with which it was tied got entangled in his horns and its neck was twisted. He got pity on the condition of the bait, so he got down, opened it and brought it back to the camp. There appeared no fowl play but his simplicity and kind heart. But this brought a bad name to the park. He was immediately transferred to Satpura National Park, Pachmarhi, with his elephant Kalyani. After some years both of them died there.

3. One day, I was sitting in my office with Mr. J.J. Dutta, our C.W.L.W., who was doing annual inspection of my office at Umaria (Bandhavgarh). Suddenly, there was a phone call from Jabalpur. Mr. Reinboth, Retd. I.C.S. and ex-Commissioner Jabalpur wanted four rooms at Tala Forest Rest House, for his and his family's stay. I told him that I was not in a position to give him the rooms on that day, because our local minister, Mr. K.P. Singh was coming from Shahdol and he may like to stay at Tala instead of Umaria. Also that as they were coming from Jabalpur only, they could very well get rooms booked with R.G.M., M.P. Tourism Development Corporation, whose office was located at Jabalpur. They could get four rooms easily in White Tiger Lodge of M.P.T.D.C., as all were vacant on that day. Mr. Dutta also agreed with my contention and reply. By lunch time, we finished with inspection work and Mr. Dutta left for Bhopal via Tala/Barhi. As I was returning to Umaria from Tala, Mr. Reinboth crossed me midway, on way to Tala. Just when I entered my office at 4.30 p.m., a call again was there from Tala. Somebody on behalf of Mr. Reinboth was again asking for rooms in F.R.H. I told him the same thing and asked him as to why did they not get it booked in white tiger lodge before leaving Jabalpur. Then he said that on way at Umaria, they had enquired at P.W.D. Rest House that the minister was going to stay at Umaria only and would not come to Tala. I said that I have not yet met anybody, first let me meet the authorities and find out the position, and then only I will give any room. Again he kept on insisting. Well! When I got fed up, I gave them only two suites, sparing two for my emergency requirement.

Now the drama starts after occupying the rooms. Mr. Reinboth called the forester Abid Khan incharge F.R.H. and baiting and said "Boda *bandho*" (tie the bait). He replied "Saheb, *pehle paise dete hain, phir boda bandhate hain*" (Sir, first payment is received in advance, then only the bait is tied). He was a bit annoyed on this and asked as to what amount was to be paid. The forester told him to pay two hundred and fifty rupees, the cost of the bait. Mr. Reinboth was taken aback and then said, "all right take these two hundred rupees, rest I will give you later on". Fr. Abid Khan told him again that full amount has to be given in advance only. Then he paid full amount and got the money receipt also from my forester. Perhaps Mr. Reinboth was expecting everything to be free. He was annoyed on refusal to give rooms of F.R.H. also. Anyway, Mr. Reinboth, coming to a National Park, had come with guns and ammunition. He called the F.G. incharge

F.R.H., Mr. Bhuvan Bhaskar Pandey and asked him to get some wild boars shot by him. The F.G. said "Sir, do not talk like this, it is not permitted and we don't do such things also". Again he said that nothing would happen, they would pay for it. Pandey avoided him and left on pretext of some work.

Next day, Mr. Reinboth saw the tigress on baiting site with his entire family. Later called Abid Khan and asked him to bring his money receipt book. He said, he wanted to write a certificate on it. That poor chap gave him the book and on that receipt he wrote that no bait was tied and no tiger was shown on the bait (in English). Mr. Abid when he took this book to the Assistant Director at Tala, to read the thing, then was it known. They were stunned that such a big man could go so low and mischievous. Not only this, when no body was there, he walked to the baiting site, lifted the head of the bait killed and two legs of the bait killed two days back. Kept these in the dickey of his car and came to Umaria at my residence. At my residence, I requested him to come inside and talk comfortably, but he refused and said he was fine out side only. I said O.K. Then he asked me about the room rent, charges for elephant ride, entrance fee, etc. He said "it is not written anywhere in the park and nobody (my staff) knew it over there". Then I told him that he was wrong and had he seen near the elephant *machan*, a big sign board with all charges displayed on it, was fixed on a stand. And that he was not the first visitor, everyday hundreds of tourists were coming to Tala and these two staff members are telling them the rates and recovering money from them, then how was he alleging like that. Then he asked as to what were the rates for tying a bait, I told him the same Rs. 250/- per bait. Then he asked me if I could recognize the remains of a fresh and an old bait. I said "Well! I am not a veterinarian, but still I can recognize it". He brought me to his car dickey, opened it, where I found a complete head with horns intact and two legs of buffalo calves. He asked me if it was a fresh bait. The head was complete, not decayed and no smell was coming from it, I said Yes! it was fresh. The legs were not clearly visible. He said, "No! it is old and I am taking it to Jabalpur Veterinary College." He closed the dickey and pushed off. He first came to the residence of Veterinary Doctor at Umaria and on not getting a reply to his satisfaction, left for Jabalpur.

4. Once in Bandhavgarh, it was around 8.30 p.m., I was getting the layout for an additional room in the Rest House kitchen. Suddenly, I found that the bait which was tied that evening in the Chorbahra site was there in front of me. For some time I could not believe it. But then it was a fact and this buffalo calf was badly mauled at the rump and was shivering out of fear. Somehow it had escaped from the clutches of our tigress and her four cubs. When I found that its condition was such that it would not survive even if

we tried for its treatment, secondly, the tigress and her cubs might be coming to that side only following this bait and some accident may not take place, I put that bait again in the trolley of my jeep and went to the baiting site. I got it tied again in the light of search light. Hardly we were back in our jeep, when all five of our tigers appeared in front of us and killed this bait in front of our eyes. Aesthetically, it was not a good sight but scientifically and administratively, it was the need of that hour.

5. In a similar incidence at Kanha, the stock of baits had exhausted at Kanha. Therefore, four baits were called, from Kisli stock. A man was moving towards Kanha on foot with these four baits. It was evening time, around 5.00 p.m. The baits were in front of the man who driving them with a stick in his hands. When he reached the base of Kanha ghat, near Salghat turning, suddenly a tiger came out of the bushes and killed one of the baits. The man hurried with remaining three, running towards Kanha, but this tiger charged again, killing one more bait. This was the moment when Mr. Pantane, Superintendent, Kanha was coming from Kanha in his jeep and almost dashed against the tiger on the road. He took a little time in understanding the situation. Then in a fraction of a minute he picked up both of the remaining baits and the man, put them in his jeep, turned around and rushed to Kanha. It was a thrilling experience and a brave act of that labour and Mr. Pantane which saved at least two of the baits at that moment. Of course, they had to be fed to the tigers only, but at a later date.

Episode-XXI

Sita: The Tigress of Bandhavgarh

As many of us know that there are a number of mythological stories, prevailing regarding Lord Rama and the Ramayana, in and around Bandhavgarh National Park. There are a number of hills and caves, which are named after many characters of Ramayana, e.g. Hanuman Manch, Sita Mandap and Bandhavgarh itself. This is the area of 'Sita Mandap', in which a female tiger was born in year 1982. The mahauts who saw it first, named it as 'Sita' only. As she grew, she occupied this territory, which was once a territory of her mother. Where had her mother gone, no body knew.

This Sita Mandap area falls in the main tourist zone of Bandhavgarh National Park. Almost all of the tourists coming to this National Park, also cover this territory during one of their morning or evening excursions. Obviously, the visibility of the local tigers also becomes a regular feature. In our parks, these tigresses become more popular, if they shed the shyness from the approach of a tourist. The reason is, once they are seen with their first litter from the back of an elephant, they are photographed to the maximum. With their young cubs, their movement is slow and restricted to a smaller area and hence are tracked easily by our elephants. Then litter after litter, these tigresses keep on obliging us with a number of memorable moments of their activities observed by the staff and the tourists both. The male tigers, barring a few are moody and cover much larger territories and hence are visible less frequently. Although some of the famous males known from Bandhavgarh are Daddy and Charger, who were also seen to the maximum and photographed also.

Sita's territory extended up to Badi gupha, Jamunia, Chor bahra, Balua *nala*, Sidh baba, Chakra dhara and Shesh shayya. Sita bore her first litter of three cubs in 1986 from a male known as Banka. Second litter from same male was born in

1989, again with three cubs. Thereafter she bore four litters from the famous tiger, the Charger in 1991 (four cubs), 1994 (two cubs) and in 1996 (two litters of three cubs each). All these years, this tigress Sita was visible to Mahauts with or without cubs. Hence it was frequently shown to the tourists also. But then she became still a famous tigress in 1996-97 as she was filmed and photographed so much by the National Geographic (U.S.) and the Partridge Films from U.K. Sita got exposure on the cover of the issue of December 1997 of National Geographic also a photographic story of this tigress. Well, this was the time when she had achieved an age of around fifteen years, old enough for a wild tigress.

This tigress Sita was seen on the last day of tourist season of 1998-99, i.e. 30th. June, 1998. Then the park was closed for rainy season up to 30th October, 1998, as a regular feature. As I said earlier, even tiger tracking is stopped for this period of four months. So you never know, where these tigers remain during these days. Even the vegetation on ground becomes very dense with tall grasses, reducing the visibility to almost zero per cent. Most of the forest roads also cut off and are un-pliable during rains. But on 20th August, 1998, I had seen this tigress with her grown up cubs near Badi gufa and that was last sighting of this tigress. When our park reopened on 1st November, 1998, Sita was not seen. Her cubs were independent now, so she was presumed to be in courtship of some male tiger again. Since the other tigers like Charger and Bachi with cubs were still visible easily, not much efforts were made to track or locate Sita. Almost one and a half months had passed. Suddenly, there appeared an article in *Navbharat* of Jabalpur, that Sita was not visible and was probably killed by some poachers during rains. The paper was very critical of the park administration and blamed me for this, said 'disappearance of this internationally famed tigress'. There was a lot of hue and cry. We were not aware of any such killing of Sita. One Mr. Lallu Singh a local self-styled leader claimed to have known the killers (some *Bahelias*, who supposed to have killed Sita with sticks, after trapping her in a "gin trap", near Jamunia area of Bandhavgarh National Park). That was the basis of this rumour. This Jamunia area is hardly one kilometre from Tala, the village and the H.Q. of Assistant Director, Range Officer and the other staff of the park and of regular range of territorial D.F.O. When I called and asked Mr. Lallu Singh, he was not sure of the date or month, even spot. When I asked as to why did he not inform then (six months back) only, he said he rang up to A.C.F. at Tala, who was not available then. Why not me, the Collector or S.P., he had no reply. He was not at all reliable. A tigress trapped in a 'gin trap' will not sit quietly. She will roar to her loudest and struggle continuously to free herself. And at a distance of about one kilometre from Tala, cannot be missed by the villagers or the staff passing nearby or even at Tala. Any body seeing a tiger in such a condition, cannot ignore it. So thereafter, the so-called poachers (*bahelias*) getting opportunity to kill it and take it away was not at all possible. It was only a rumour being spread to malign the name of park and

Fig. 21.1: Shesh shayya, the Statue of Lord Vishnu of Tenth Century

Fig. 21.2: Tigress Sita's Cub at Bandhavgarh

Fig. 21.3: Charger—The Famous Tiger of Bandhavgarh

Fig. 21.4: Daughter of Sita in Chakradhara, Bandhavgarh

Fig. 21.5: Bandhavgarh Hill from Rajbahra, Bandhavgarh

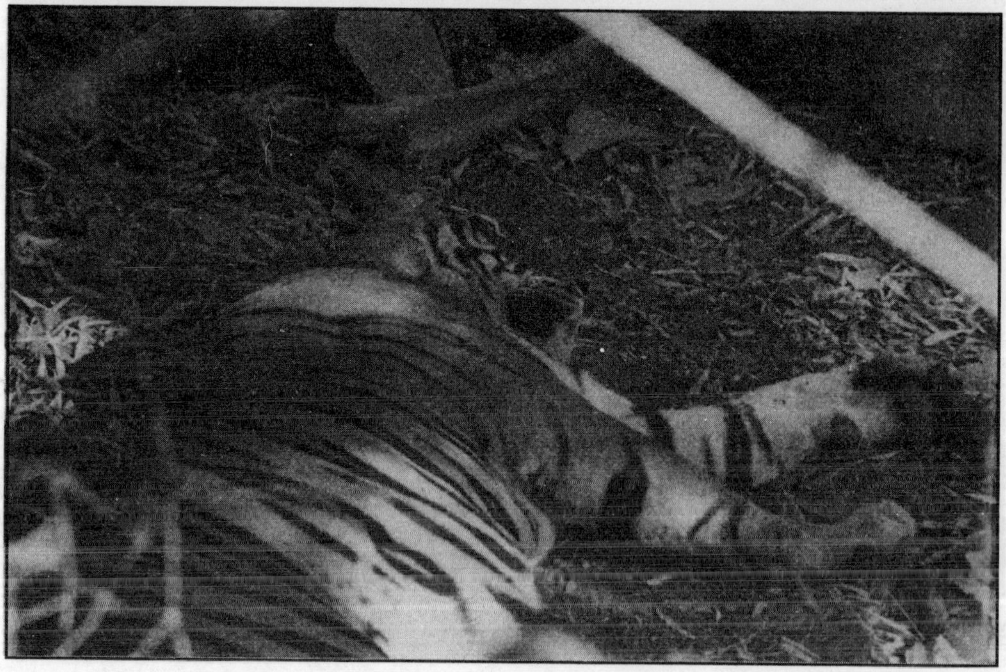

Fig. 21.6: Sita, the Tigress During her Last Few Months

Fig. 21.7: Sita's Daughter Bachi with the Cub

Fig. 21.8: Sita's Daughter Bachi with the Cub

me, with a definite motive. The local press people wanted to blackmail me, they wanted money which I never gave. The local M.L.A. was annoyed due to same very vested interest. The other local forest officer, who was my subordinate earlier at Balaghat, was charged sheeted by me for his indisciplined behaviour, was perhaps instigating the M.L.A. against me and obliging this M.L.A. This M.L.A. of Umaria was now having only one aim that is to shift me from Bandhavgarh. So he started levelling all base less charges against me. A long list of complaints, for which P.C.C.F. (Wildlife) and even Commissioner Rewa came to enquire into. Although nothing happened of those complaints, as they were all baseless and totally false, but the M.L.A. left no stage unused to bark against me and the park. Call attention motion in the assembly was replied by the then Forest Minister himself, I was not needed to brief him in this issue.

Ultimately, during his visit to Bandhavgarh, the then Chief Minister, M.P. also asked me about this episode of Sita. He asked me, how were they saying that she was killed in a 'gin trap'. Then I told him clearly that yes! it is possible to trap a tiger in a gin trap and then kill it, but then evidence is required to prove it or action to be taken. In the beginning of my service, in year 1966, I had seen one tiger in gin trap in Sontalai P.F., between Itarsi and Bagra Tawa railway stations. It kept on roaring for almost twelve hours and so loudly that it was audible as far as 1-2 kilometres distance. It was finally shot by the then Collector, Hoshangabad, Mr. Ramnath Singh, in front of us only. But in this case, all complaints were just imaginations of Lallu Singh and his party. I told the C.M. that if they can show me the exact spot, where they are claiming to have been killed, still I will find out the evidence of a tiger having been killed there. He asked me what was that, I said 'hair', I may find some fallen hair of Sita, still lying there and we can identify it under the microscope and at least confirm the happening. But these people are not in a position to show me that also. If they had seen it being killed six months back, why were they acting like a mute spectator only. Why did not they try to stop the crime and inform me or if not me, the Collector or S.P. He was convinced. But then our M.L.A. made it a prestige issue and ultimately, got me transferred from Bandhavgarh.

There were speculations and the reply from my side as follows:

1. Sita was quite old and might have died a natural death.
2. She might have left the territory and moved to some other area. Her territory was occupied by one of her daughters.
3. Might have been killed by some other adult tiger, during rainy season.
4. Might have really been killed by some poachers.

The first possibility was in my view, much stronger. Till then the longest age of known wild tiger was 18 years and that too of a male in Royal Chitwan Park in Nepal. Our Sita was about sixteen years, which was mature enough and she was bidding good-bye at this age. But then the question arose as to where had the body gone. Those of us who have seen wildlife and the forest, know that the cats have a very peculiar behaviour of going to very remote and secluded, even unapproachable places, before they are just going to die. That is the reason, why the dead bodies of most of the tigers are never found in the forest. This question was asked in Project Tigers Millennium meeting at Delhi also, that assuming the tiger population in India to be around 3000 and animal's death rate of 10 per cent in a natural way, then 300 dead bodies of the tigers should be found in the forests only. Why is it so that we find hardly 30-40 bodies in whole of the country. Repy by some of the experts was given the same. Some years back when Mr. Hasan was Director in Bandhavgarh National Park, there was a severe fight between two tigers. The loser was fatally injured also. Mr. Hasan followed it with the help of elephants and when they located it, it was about to enter a small circular opening of a cave. They tried to stop it from entering it but it still entered that hole and vanished inside, not at all visible from outside. Then they put a long bamboo in side and disturbed it, in order to force it out. It came out, but then succumbed to its injuries after about an hour's time. Had they not seen it entering that small hole, nobody could have ever imagined that a full grown tiger had gone in side through such a small hole and died inside. What of dead body?

Secondly, the scavenging system of the forest is so fast that one can hardly find a body or bones of a dead animal after a few days. Here I remember one scene of Kanha. I was returning from Bamhnidadar, when I saw about 8-10 wild dogs drinking water in Shrawan taal. Time was aroud 11.00 a.m. Late Commodore Sanjana of Mukki was behind me in his jeep. We were quietly watching the activity of these wild dogs. After drinking water they moved towards main meadows and suddenly caught one young chital stag on the road itself. We were still waiting and seeing the entire scene of chital being pulled down, tearing, sharing, eating, etc. Simultaneously, the vultures and jackals also started moving to the spot and one would not believe, just within fifteen minutes time there was nothing left. One could not find any remains of that chital, everything was gone, except a few blood stains on the road. Myself and Mr. Sanjana looked at each others face, smiled and moved on our way.

The second possibility could not be confirmed as Sita was not seen on search in any of the adjoining areas of the park. Actually Sita after becoming adult had occupied her mother's territory and so was done by one of her daughters. It is generally a rule that male replaces a male's territory and the female replaces a female's.

The third possibility of having been killed by other tiger was also quite strong. Some people believe that an adult tiger cannot be killed by any other animal, even other tigers. But that is not true. The tigers do kill other adult tigers and even eat the carcass. Once during our International Workshop on wildlife management at Kanha in 1981, one huge male tiger was killed by another tiger near Deotalai camp and its half eaten body was brought at Kanha and shown to all experts. So such conflicts are possible for territory or mate, when they may fight to kill each other and then eat. In Sita's case, no such evidence was found, it was only a guess.

The fourth and the last thing which could have happened, was killing by some poachers. National parks are not having any air tight boundaries. They are neither fenced, walled nor protected by any such means, where people cannot enter it. The boundary is open on all sides. During rains, when tourist vehicle movement is also stopped, poachers can enter quite easily from anywhere, avoiding the notice of patrolling parties and then indulge in such activities. But still unless one catches them or at least some evidence is there, we cannot do anything. The rumours were there, but with no concrete evidence, so it was also ruled out.

Making Sita's disappearance an issue was for my shifting only. Otherwise why could not they find out Sita till now, even after six years. Had she been killed by poachers, why could they not prove it till now, I was not there to hinder any enquiry. Sita still remains a mystery. After this episode we learnt that we should never name these wild tigers. Let them remain tigers and tigresses only, not Sita, Charger or Bachi. These tigers are not immortal, they also die after certain age due to various reasons. Who will keep on replying to such baseless allegations. In Bandhavgarh National Park, it is customary to give a shock to the director each year, when it opens first for the tourists. Once earlier also, I was told in the first week of November, 1997 by our minister I/c district, that the Charger has been shot by some poachers during rains. Immediately, I sent my mahauts in search of Charger and there it was alive, hale and hearty. Some people, sitting there at Delhi in air conditioned rooms, think that they are the only custodians of tigers, and those who are there in the field, are justifiers, irresponsible and careless people. They must keep in mind that the officers at the rank of Directors, Deputy Directors and Assistant Directors are very responsible officers. They also love this fascinating animal as much as any other tiger lover of the country. Before making an opinion, based on their own sources, they must ask for first hand information from the persons, who are fighting against all odds in protecting our tigers.

Episode-XXII

The Leopard of Bamhni-dadar

It was an evening in Kanha National Park. Myself, Dr. P.C. Kotwal, Mr. V.B. Sawarkar and Mr. Shaikh from Melghat Tiger Reserve were busy listening to the recorded tapes of the speeches given by delegates of various countries, during the first International Symposium on tiger. Actually we acted as 'rapporteurs' during the symposium and were then asked to finalize the minutes of this symposium. The dialects of the Chinese and other South-East Asian countries were such that hardly we could understand in first go. So we had to replay a number of times to listen and then transcript rightly. It was very tiring and boring job. That was the time, when we were having two leopard cubs at Kanha, Sulkum and Maikal. They were quite grown up by that time and were very playful. Every visitor to Kanha had this as an added attraction for him.

Mr. Sawarkar had come with his family also. We took a little break and decided to have a round up to Bamhni-dadar to refresh ourselves. In my open jeep, I was driving and Mrs. Sawarkar and children were sitting with me in the front seats. Mr. Sawarkar, Mr. Shaikh, Dr. Kotwal and the driver were sitting behind us. After a round of Kanha meadows, we were moving towards Bamhni-dadar. It was late evening in mid of *ghat* road. Suddenly, a leopard, apparently a female and adult appeared in front of the jeep, right in the centre of the road. Everybody was thrilled. Yes! the leopard is certainly the most beautiful animal in the forest. It just crossed the road slowly and moved downwards on right side of the ghat road. We halted there for some moments, talked about it and again proceeded. After a furlong or so, again a leopard, slightly bigger and perhaps a male was sitting in a crouching position, right in the centre again. Aye! what is this. It was a fearless animal, budging not an inch on approach of our jeep. I stopped my jeep at about ten feet distance, everybody quietly observing it. This leopard was repeatedly touching its nostrils on the ground at one particular place and smelling something. What a sight! After about two to three minutes time, it got up and moved on right side (valley side) of the ghat road. By then the sun had just set and it was getting little dark. We could not see the animal in the grass of road side now. I switched on the light, turned my jeep towards right to see it again in the head light. And then our leopard was again out on the road. This time it started coming towards our jeep. Everybody got panicky, especially the wife and children of Mr. Sawarkar. I whispered and told everybody not to be afraid of. It would not say anything, if we kept quiet. It was coming on right side (drivers side), walking very leisurely, undisturbed, just straight down the slope. Then it went past my jeep, just brushing its body with the footboard of my jeep. Had I wanted could have patted its back also. After our jeep, it started walking in the centre of the road, downwards.

Now everybody was relaxed after this thrilling experience and could realize that the female which passed that spot, must have sprayed in the centre of the road. This male on getting scent of the female pheromones was approaching her. We and our jeep was becoming an obstruction between them. This male was not at all concerned about us. It only wanted its "right of passage" towards the female. It was after all their domain. For some time, we were thinking as if our Sulkum and Maikal had escaped from Kanha and reached that spot. But this was a memorable experience of life.

Fig. 24.1: One of the Cubs of New Litter, Still with Closed Eyes

Fig. 24.2: The Tigress Carrying her Cub, Holding in her Mouth

Fig. 24.3: The Older Cub on the Goat Kill

Fig. 24.4: The Tigress at New Site with Her Older Cub

Fig. 24.5: Tigress with Both Litters

Fig. 24.6: Both Litters Feeding at the same Time

Fig. 24.7: Both Litters Feeding at the Same Time

Episode-XXIII

Visit of Mr. Haji Inayat the Minister for Jails, M.P.

While in Bandhavgarh, during 1980-82, it was an evening of March, 1981. I was sitting with my family in a relaxing mood. There at Umaria, one Thakur is supposed to be possessed by a saintly soul of one '*peer baba*' during the days of Muharram. Every year he was supposed to be in such a condition for two to three days. Many people from far away places throng in at Umaria, to get blessings from this soul. They ask this soul about their personal doubts and with the blessings, their wishes are fulfilled. That was also a Muharram day. Suddenly, SDO, Umaria's message was there that Mr. Haji Inayat, the Minister for Jails, M.P. Government was there in the town and wanted to see me. I went immediately. He asked me if he along with his family could take a round of park. They had come from Jabalpur, to take blessings of Baba' (locally called as "*Murad maangna*") and now wanted to take a round of the park also. I said, "Sir, now it is already dark and the visibility is very poor, you won't see any animal. He said, "you can show with the help of search light". I informed him that we do not use the search light. Secondly, our park also closed after sun set. He insisted on, saying he was the minister in the State Government and can inspect anything at anytime. Well, I had to yield to his pressures, but I said, "you will have to come in my jeep only and no other vehicle can come inside." He agreed for that. Then the Minister and his wife sat with me in the front seat. At the back seat were sitting, two of his college going daughters and the driver. The sun had already set. By the time we entered the park, it was around 8.00 p.m. In the headlights of the jeep only those animals can be seen which come across the road. The time was such an odd one that even all grazing animals like Chitals had settled in the meadows by now. From Tala to Rajbahra, not a single animal was seen, during this drive of about ten kilometres distance.

They were cursing the park, suddenly two hares were seen on the road. The girls were very critical and made a mockry of it by calling them as 'tigers'. In my heart, I was cursing them also. It was not a time of seeing wildlife. Sunrise or the dusk time is the best, but what could they expect at 8.30 p.m.

We reached Bathan village, in the centre of the park (a deserted and relocated village site), at about 9.00 p.m. The entire drive was almost a blank. Then I thought of taking a longer route while returning. Coming back via Damna, Bheetari side around the Bandhavgarh hill is around 30 kms. After fifteen minutes drive on the out skirts of Damna village, a huge male tiger was seen standing on the right side of the road. I stopped the jeep at about ten feet distance from it. The lord of the jungle did not move and kept standing for a few minutes. The minister whispered, *"Dar lag raha hai, gaadi peechhe le lijiye"*. Then repeated his daughters behind. In open jeep, seeing a tiger so close was not being pleasant for them. Then I cautioned them neither to talk nor to move, else it would catch that person only. If otherwise it wished to attack, it would attack me first, as I am the closest to it. My tiger obliged me and then moved towards Damna village. After that, these two girls, who were talking too much, were like dead ones. Even our minister and his wife did not utter a word during our further drive of forty-five minutes. At Tala F.R.H., they all immediately rushed to the toilets and then got into their car and buzzed off to Jabalpur. Perhaps they had spoiled their clothes out of fear.

One should never force the park officials, whether a minister or the bureaucrats, to see these sacred parks of old times, violating our rules and norms. After all we are there to show you the wild animals. If you stick to the time suggested by park officials, you are bound to see maximum number of animals, to your satisfaction. Once late Mr. S.S. Buit, the retired C.C.F., Maharashtra had come to Kanha, with his wife and children. After three days stay, when they had seen maximum number of tigers and other animals, Mrs. Buit called me and said "Sharma, I went on almost all tours with Mr. Buit during his forty years service and then ten years after retirement, but never had seen a tiger. Now here, you are the first officer who has shown me not only my first but so many tigers during one visit".

For seeing a tiger in the forest or a National Park, one must have a luck also. During the times, when baiting was prevalent in M.P. parks, once a foreign dignitary (a guest of our Chief Wildlife Warden) had come to Kanha from England. Now to show them the tiger in their two days stay at Kanha, we tried our best. Even tied three baits, at three different sites. On second night all three baits were killed, but the tigers did not stop at the kills. So we could not show any tigers. They had to be satisfied with photography of our beloved leopards, Sulkum and Maikal. They were not disappointed, as they themselves were wildlife officers and knew well that we cannot dictate terms to the wild tigers. It is their will to stop or not to stop for a show to the visitors. It is my belief also that in a park, if a tiger is being seen, one must honour it and must see it, if informed. If you disrespect it, it will then never appear before you. Once at Bandhavgarh, our Conservator of Forest, Shahdol

Territorial Circle was coming to Manpur for some inspection. That day six full grown tigers (mother, father and four cubs) were located on a kill. My elephants were kept ready at the site. I stopped the C.F. at Tala and requested him to see these tigers, a rare sight. But he was least interested and preferred to go straight to Manpur for coupe inspection. It would have taken hardly half an hour for him to see the tigers. He said "some other time I will see the tigers". O.K., I had no reply then. After many years, when he retired and was staying at Jabalpur, he again came to Bandhavgarh, during my second tenure. This time, he was with his daughter and son-in-law also. Now when during two days stay, they could not see a tiger, he said "Sharma, we will not go back till we see a tiger". I told him that because he did not stop for tigers while going to Manpur on that day, the tigers are not obliging us now. Somehow, I could show him our tigress Sita, that evening behind Badi gufa area and they were really thrilled to see this majestic animal.

One day, during our International Workshop on Wildlife Management, at Kanha, myself and Mr. S.M. Hasan were waiting for the elephants very early morning. It was bitter cold that day. The elephant which first came back from the tiger spot, was having the same gentleman on its back, as our P.C.C.F. On seeing us he said, "*tum logon ka pet sher dekh ke bhara nahin abhi*" (you both are yet not satisfied after seeing so many tigers for the last so many years). We said, "No sir, we will see every tiger, whenever it is seen. It is such a fascinating animal that one cannot afford to miss it".

Episode-XXIV

The Tigress with Two Litters

Once a tigress near Badi Chuhari area of Kanha National Park, delivered three cubs in the year 1986. But somehow two cubs died very young. The third one, a male cub was also not very healthy. This cub kept on clinging to its mother for survival. When the cub was about five months old, the mahauts reported that they had seen perhaps the same female mating with the dominating male of the Chuhari area. They could not see the cub that day. After about four months time, one day I was sitting in Kanha, when the mahauts informed me that they had seen the tigress with newly born litter of four cubs and that the last cub of the last litter was also there seen with her. I immediately rushed to the area and was surprised to see our tigress moving her new born cubs to a new site. These cubs had not opened their eyes even. This male cub of last litter and of about eight months age was also on its heels. We kept on following her and at one very difficult spot, I was astonished and worried also to see that the new born cubs were suckling their mother, so also was this large eight months old cub. She was permitting both. Actually, this older cub was also not in good shape, it appeared very thin and lean and perhaps was starving for some days. It came to my mind that if this older cub also kept on suckling its mother, the entire milk would be sucked by it only and the younger cubs would then also starve. Apparently, the tigress had not hunted for some days and was also hungry. I thought of feeding them, artificially but seeing the terrain and the spot, it was not possible to reach there with a bigger animal fast. And secondly, she was shifting the site very frequently. I rushed back to Kanha on the elephant, keeping others at the site only. I searched for a big goat at Kanha labour camp, luckily, I got one and brought it back. The moment I lowered this goat, our tigress caught hold of it and killed it instantaneously and then I saw her and her older cub feeding heartily. It was very satisfying. Next day, we could not locate this tigress as it perhaps had moved to very remote and precipitous terrain. A day earlier I had fed those hungry mother and the cub, but this cub could not sustain longer. After some days, it was found abandoned by its mother, injured and struggling for life on a fire line near Kanha. Ultimately, it succumbed to its injuries very soon.

This was a unique case, where this tigress came into oestrus very soon and also mated with the male and bore another litter. Generally a tigress with cubs does not come into oestrus till this first litter gains adulthood and weans out, roughly say two years time. But if all cubs die earlier, it may come into oestrus immediately after that. That is why in various zoos, the cubs are removed from mother much earlier and are hand reared. Then this mother comes in oestrus, producing cubs at a much shorter cycle. But there in nature, while a cub of last litter is still with the mother, her coming into oestrus is a rare phenomenon. Sometimes these tigresses with young cubs do entice the males approaching, to divert their attention from her cubs, so that those cubs are safe and are not killed by the larger males. It may be a fake love affair, but becoming physically fit for next progeny is really rare. Some experts say that even when a tigress has all sick cubs and is hopeless about their survival, may lose interest in these cubs and may come into oestrus again and mate with male to give a better and healthy litter to the nature.

These scenes were photographed by a Japanese photographer also and perhaps were shown on Japan T.V. in "Waku Waku Wonderland" programme for children.

Episode-XXV

The Huge Tiger of Panna with Big Beard

When I was Director, Panna National Park, one day our Commissioner, Sagar Division, Mr. G.S. Sahni came for his first meeting with the District Officers. He was very glad to see me almost after eight years. Way back in 1978-80, when I was Deputy Director, Kanha Tiger Reserve, Mr. Sahni was Collector, Mandla. We had good rapport and friendship at Mandla. After the meeting, he said that next day after inspection of Tahsil office he would like to take a round of Panna National Park. It was his first visit of this park. I said O.K. and then he told me to wait for him at my residence, whenever he returned from inspection, he would come direct and then we go to the park.

Next day, I was waiting at my residence, at about 3.00 p.m., he came to my residence and said that they were quite late now, as they had to go back to Sagar also. So he wanted to postpone his visit for the next time. I said, "why to postpone, you are late by one hour, so we will take a smaller round of the park this time. Time-wise one hour short trip. He agreed and we came to Panna National Park via Hinauta. We changed over to my open gypsy, I was driving and Mr. Sahni was sitting with me in the front seat. One Mr. Mandal, an I.A.S. probationer, my Range Officer, Mr. S.N. Singh and the driver were sitting behind on the back seats. We took a quick round and came to 'Dhundua seha', the sunset point at a water fall, so as to reach there just before the sunset.

After seeing the sunset, as we were thinking of returning back, Mr. Lokendra Singh, the ex-Maharajkumar of Panna came from Hinauta side and told us to go quickly towards that up hill side, as there was a big herd of Sambars to see, right on the road. We rushed towards that point. In this area, the road is very narrow (just jeep width) with very thick jungle and dense undergrowth. As we completed the one kilometre long ascent, there was a small open patch on right side. Mr. Singh, my R.O. was looking for the Sambar herd, which was not there. It was getting dark now. I was busy in driving, while looking mostly in front only. So also was Mr. Sahni. As we passed by that open patch, suddenly Mr. Singh and Mr. Mandal started shouting "drive the vehicle fast". From that open patch, they had seen a huge male tiger coming on the road and then chasing our gypsy. I raised speed a little, and then at some distance stopped and looked back. I could also see the tiger, which now was standing in the middle of the road. After a second, it again returned to that open patch. Mr. Sahni could not see it, because by the time he turned back, it was gone.

It was a strange behaviour. Never had seen a tiger chasing a vehicle. Mr. Sahni had accompanied us in Kanha on several occasions and had seen the tigers very closely, even during one tranquillizing exercise also. So he was also very curious about this tiger. We thought of going back and see it again. I moved my vehicle in reverse gear only, right up to that point, where tiger was seen standing on the road. It was quite dark now and we could see the tiger nowhere around us. Everybody's eyes were searching for it. I put my lights on. Here we were getting that typical cattish smell, which was familiar to Mr. Sahni also. Mr. Sahni stood on the front seat also but could not locate the tiger anywhere. Then I put the search light on, which was fitted on the right side upper corner of my vehicle. As I moved it a little right side, "my God!", that big tiger which was sitting behind a tendu tree, just on right side of the road and hardly at a distance of five feet from my gypsy, stood up. I reversed my vehicle further to reach comparatively a safer distance. Now this tiger moved again, taking almost full round of this open patch. Finding a clear distance in front, I moved my vehicle, keeping my eyes on the road only. Others were keeping their eyes on tiger only. A huge old male, with a big mane and beard. Suddenly once again, all started shouting at me to race the vehicle fast, because this tiger of ours once again had come on the road and started running towards our gypsy. Well! I moved fast. It stopped chasing and then escaped into the dense forest cover. We came back. Mr. Sahni was also a bit scared this time and said, "Sharma, we were doomed today." I said, "No sir, not exactly". It was really first experience of its type. Next day, when I enquired from mahauts of our elephants, they said that this was big male tiger with very bad temperament and even used to chase away our elephants also.

This gave a fame to Panna National Park, through Mr. Sahni also. Till now the Panna N.P. was not for tiger sighting. Next Sunday, Mr. Sahni fixed a meeting of all Collectors of the Division at Panna and asked me to show tiger to them also. I said that the tiger is not waiting for us there only, we cannot promise, but certainly we will try our best. As the luck would have it, not that male tiger, but a female was shown moving on the road in broad day light, over a distance of one kilometre to the accompanying Collectors of Sagar (Mr. P.S. Tomar) and Damoh, Mr. Aggarwal. She was very docile and obliged us with her memorable activities.

This male tiger of ours was not known to have chased any vehicle any other day. But that day's chasing made everybody sweat with a life long unforgettable experience.

Episode-XXVI

The Wandering Crocodiles of Shivpuri Lake

Those who have seen Shivpuri, know that the Madhav National Park is just adjacent to the township and is surrounded on three sides by the city itself. Even the entrance gate at sailing club is hardly three kilometres from the main market of the city. There are two big lakes inside the park, the Sakhya sagar and the Madhav sagar. Both are man-made and were constructed by the late Maharaja Sir Madhav Rao Scindia in 1918. These lakes are having a good number of Crocodiles in them. Up streams the Sakhya Sagar lake is connected by a *nala* which leads to the Shivpuri town and pours all dirty water in the lake. During summer, there is hardly any flow in this *nala*, but during rains, a lot of water is seen gushing into the lake.

It is this time during rains that many crocodiles move through this *nala* and come to the town. There are a number of ponds situated in the Shivpuri town. Once these crocodiles reach these ponds, many of them start living there only. In 1983, when I was Director, Madhav National Park, a crocodile was supposed to have occupied one of such ponds and had eaten two asses also, which were grazing near the pond. As the water receded, these crocodiles used to move back to the lake, probably through the same route of *nala*.

Once in summer, at about 2.00 p.m., I got a funny information that one crocodile was moving on the road side, along the rubble wall of the road side plantation. Immediately, I moved with my staff and equipments. It was really a sight to look at. A full grown up crocodile was sitting along the rubble wall, avoiding hot sun. It was quite agile. The nearest water point was about two kilometres away. Till then, I had never caught any crocodile. Therefore, I had to depend on my experienced staff, who had done this type of work several times earlier also. We had a small cage of welded wire mesh, long enough to contain a crocodile. A tractor trolley to

Fig. 26.1: The Crocodile near Rubble wall of the Plantation

Fig. 26.2: The Crocodile with Covered Eyes, an Attempt to Drive it into the Cage

Fig. 26.3: Crocodile Finally in the Cage

Fig. 26.4: Crocodile being Carried to the Lake for Release

carry the same. The other equipment consisted mainly of ropes, gunny bags and long poles with forks on the top. The crocodile was very agile and was attacking us on approach, snapping its wide mouth in quick succession. It was turning around also very swiftly.

Now the first thing was to tie its snout, so that it could not hurt us by snapping its mouth. This cannot be done unless the animal is quiet and approachable. For that, first of all we had to cover its eyes, so that it could not see any human being coming near it. Next we took a big gunny bag, hooked it on the top of a long bamboo, slowly brought it on the top of the head of the crocodile and left it slowly to drop it on its eyes, covering full view. Now once it was blind, it did not move at all. Now with two long forked poles, we fixed the animal to the ground, one fork at the neck joint and the other at the pelvic joint. I was astonished to see that this animal could now be handled very easily. A loop of the rope was put on the snout and on tightening it, closed its mouth shut and fixed. Then it was a matter of a few minutes. Hardly three persons from our staff coolly directed it to enter the cage, then on to the tractor trolley and back to our lake.

I got this animal released into the lake by our senior most officer, Mr. G.S. Bhatt, the then Director, Forest School, Shivpuri. Once more a crocodile was caught from the Shivpuri town, simply put in the tractor trolley and then got it released by late Mr. Madhav Rao Scindia, who was there in the town on that day. It was a good experience, as capturing a crocodile without tranquillizing gun or drug and with the help of simple equipments was new to me.

Once earlier at Mandla, when I was Deputy Director, Kanha in 1979, we got an information that a crocodile entered a village nearby and was caught by the villagers. It had gone from river Narmada along with flood waters. When myself and Mr. H.S. Panwar reached the village, we found that the villagers had trapped the crocodile under a big log of tree. It could not escape under its weight. We put a loop of the rope around its snout and closed its mouth, then putting cotton straps around its fore and hind legs just lifted it into our vehicle and brought it to Mandla. We kept it in a small pond of our office. We tried to feed it with fish but it never ate anything. There was a big wound in its neck region, perhaps created by some sharp edged weapon by the villagers, while overpowering it. Due to this wound, it could not gulp anything. For one week, our Veterinary Doctor of Mandla gave a number of injections but could not cure or improve the condition, ultimately it died.

But catching a crocodile with the help of forked poles, gunny bags and ropes was an experience in itself.

Episode-XXVII

The Spoiled Lad Indrajit

We know that when first child is born in a family, we love and pamper it so much that sometimes he gets spoiled due to it. Similarly, when the elephants started breeding in our elephant camp at Bandhavgarh, the first few calves got a lot of love and care, both by the mahauts and the elephants. One of such early born calves was Indrajit, a male elephant, which has grown very tall, majestic and handsome. It has come out to be a beautiful elephant, very healthy and very tall. But as I said, it is a little spoiled, some due to love and affection and some due to his own power of youth. With time, it was also taken into the squad of tourist elephants. It started carrying tourists for the park round and the tiger show. But due to its '*masti*', it was in habit of pushing other elephants, chasing them to hit or to play with them. When will it come in that mood, you never know.

On one such occasion, when some tourists were climbing up another elephant from a gypsy, this Indrajit elephant was standing nearby in waiting for its turn. Suddenly he pushed the other elephant with such a force that this elephant fell on the gypsy. Luckily no tourist was hurt but certainly the front one side door, seat and the bonnet of the gypsy were badly damaged and bent due to the weight of the elephant. Later the gypsy owner had come to me to claim the damages (which were never shown to me). Due to the indemnity certificate nothing was paid to him.

In another incident, Mr. Vidya Charan Shukla had come to Bandhavgarh. Second day, his security staff had gone for park round on one elephant. The moment they returned and entered the campus of the Rest House, Indrajit, which was also standing in the campus with its mahaut on, started chasing this elephant, dashing in full speed. The mahaut of the other elephant could sense the danger in time and also started moving his elephant fast. Now there was an elephant race in the campus. The mahaut of the elephant with security staff started running his elephant to save it from Indrajit's attack. Indrajit was following it on full speed with its mahaut having almost no control on it. It was scene to look at. Everybody was running helter scalter, trying to save his own life. The security staff was thinking that they are gone now. They were shouting from the back of the elephant and trying to hold the hauda fast so that they did not fall from it. I ordered the mahaut to take the elephant out of the campus. Then both of the elephants came out on the road, Indrajit chasing the other for about a kilometre on Tala-Umaria road. Then only it stopped and turned into the nearby forest and the elephant with security staff could return to the camp. Luckily all safe but shaken badly. Mr. V.C. Shukla and his security staff left early next morning never to return again, till I was there.

In July 1999, I was transferred to Pench Tiger Reserve, Seoni. On reaching there, I was informed that my predecessor had asked for elephants from Satpuda National Park and that one male, one female with a calf were already half way and had reached Chhindwara. Because, there are no sufficient Bamboo patches in Pench for the elephants to feed on during the night, I had earlier refused to send elephants from Bandhavgarh. I was sure, they would starve in Pench. But now they got it from Satpuda. So they were there in Pench also for the first time. Yes! There is no Bamboo or tall grasses for the elephants to graze in Pench National Park. So the elephants have to depend on leaves and the branches of the trees, hence, all the smaller trees are felled by them to feed on leaves, thereby damaging a lot of forest area around their camps.

Anyway, we started using these elephants also for tracking tigers in Pench as well. By the end of first tourist season, we located one tigress with two young cubs. It was seen by the entire staff and one tourist party also. This female was acclimatized with the approach of elephants and started stopping for the visitors. Next year, our local M.L.A. became our Minister of Forest Department and started insisting on getting more elephants from Kanha and Bandhavgarh National Parks. I protested as there was no sufficient fodder, especially during summer, but on his own he ordered from the top. So we got two elephants from Kanha and two from Bandhavgarh, which included this Indrajit also.

The young calf of the first female from Satpuda, died one day from some unknown disease during rains. Poor mother was very sad. She was very docile elephant. One evening, as she returned to the camp, after evening round of the tourists, this brute Indrajit came running to her, dashed her with force and made her to fall on the ground. And then pierced his one long tusk into her throat. With great difficulty, it was pushed away. This tusk made a big hole in her neck, which opened in the buccal cavity. She was bleeding badly. The mahaut made her to stand and informed our Veterinary Doctor (Dr. Vyas). He came and did some dressing and gave her a few bottles of Saline. I informed Dr. A.B. Shrivastava, Head of the Wildlife Health Wing at Veterinary College, Jabalpur, who promised to come next day. Actually the condition of the elephant was such, that whatever was being fed to her was coming out of this hole, even water. So we were very much worried. Indrajit was tied with a tree under shade as punishment and also to let him cool down.

Next day, Dr. A.B. Shrivastava came with one more surgeon and operated upon our elephant by 12.00 noon. They were very cautious, because this area is full of fine nerves also. They reached to the maximum depth that could be reached, cleaned and sutured with a hope that it would work. Our Dr. Vyas was then dressing her wound and giving her injections prescribed by them. Her condition kept on deteriorating, as she could neither feed nor drink water. Third day Dr. Vyas informed me that all her ear veins were blocked and no more glucose/saline could be given. I started getting sugarcane from Jamatara village of Chhindwara side to feed her, so that whatever little juice could go inside would help her retain some energy.

Next evening, I was sitting at my residence when Dr. Vyas came running, clearly upset. I was a bit disturbed. He was with a glass jar and showed it to me, saying "Sir, the wound was healing from out side but suddenly she has thrown the entire tissue and now still a bigger hole has been formed. A very big gape. "Again I informed Dr. Shrivastava. We were worried about the life of this elephant. I suggested to send this elephant to Jabalpur to the Veterinary College, where better care could be given by other Doctors also. After taking consent from the Dean, I sent the elephant by truck to the Veterinary College, along with its mahaut and our Dr. Vyas.

On first night, our elephant Sarasvati was kept in a big hall with so many windows and one door. It was supposed to be a 'Hathikhana' of the Veterinary College. She was neither chained nor fixed to the peg or something. The mahaut also slept somewhere else. In the middle of the night, she started getting restless, alone in this hall and in a new environment. She started moving inside the hall, trying to come out through windows/door. She shook all their windows, ultimately, broke open the door and came out. Pulled the water supply line of the nearby quarters. Then only her activities were noticed and she was controlled and taken away by the mahaut. Then she was tied with the chain to a big tree in the campus. Later on, the Dean asked me to compensate for the damages done by our elephant. We sent our Range Officer to get the things repaired suitably.

When the treatment was required, there was some confusion. One Doctor from Surgery Department refused to take up, the H.O.D. left on leave. Again the Dean was contacted. Then he formed a committee of four to five Doctors, who were to carry out surgery and the treatment. In one week's time, there was not much improvement. We were feeding her with sugarcane only. Then one day, Dean called me to Jabalpur to attend the meeting of treatment committee. They were actually not sure of her survival and were having only 50 per cent hope, so they asked me to take away the elephant, back to forest and their Doctors were to come and attend her once a week. Perhaps they were thinking that if she died in the forest, at least their Veternary College would not get a bad name. They even asked me to consult any other expert from other states also for her treatment. They gave me the address of one Doctor from Assam also for this purpose. I knew of Dr. Krishnamurty of Tamil Nadu, who is a retired Veterinary Doctor from Tamil Nadu Eorest Department. Somehow I got his telephone number from Dr. Rajesh Gopal, the then F.D.P.T., Kanha and rang him up. Dr. Krishnamurty was then going to some South-East Asian country, that day only for fifteen days tour, so he was unable to come to Jabalpur before that. But he asked for the condition and symptoms on phone only and as per his experience suggested for dressing with Silver nitrate and giving retaining sutures only. He was sure that she would recover in that way only. So I insisted to keep our elephant there at the Veterinary College only and giving this suggested treatment. One Dr. Pandey, H.O.D. surgery department took special care and interest and then with this line of treatment she recovered completely and is still surviving. Thanks ultimately to the staff of Veterinary College, Jabalpur and the Dean, who was also equally concerned.

Episode-XXVIII

A Collector with Difference

When I was Director, Madhav National Park, Shivpuri between 1982-84, I was fortunate to have one Collector, by name Mr. M.P. Rajan. A real down to earth man, always helping the right persons. He was very eco-friendly and loved my National Park and its wildlife. He used to plan developing this park and tourism on the lines of Haryana tourism. He used to say "Sharma leave your park on me, I will take care of its protection side". Almost every night, he used to come after dinner and sit at Sailing club for a few hours. Once miscreants know that the Collector is sitting inside, they dared not venture into the lake or the park. Ms. Asha Gopal, the S.P. also rendered a lot of help during this period. It was a very co-operative team.

One day, on 27-3-1983, I had just returned from the park at about 7.00 p.m. The driver was gone and I was taking out my shoes, when a peon informed me that there was a call for me at D.F.O's. residence, the third bungalow from mine (that time I did not have a phone at my residence). When I went there, D.F.O. said that a Forest Guard Karan Singh was calling from Sailing club and was saying that he was assaulted by one Sardarji with a *'Pharsa'* (a sharp edged weapon) on his thigh and needed immediate help. When I tried to contact back at the Sailing club, he was not available. Now, it was not clear as to what exactly had happened, the reason for assault, how many persons were there, etc. Unless I went to the spot, nothing was going to be clear, but then I needed the Range Officer and the other staff to help me in emergency. Immediately I took out my jeep, first came to the Range colony, took R.O. and the other staff and straight came to the Sailing club. The staff over there said that F.G. Karan Singh was attacked by a Sardarji with *Pharsa* on his thigh and was bleeding. And that he had gone in Collector's jeep towards Jhansi. Nothing more did he know.

I did not know, what to do. The Range Officer informed me that Karan Singh was posted at Gate No. 6. So we went there, thinking to get some information over there, but nothing. Again we came back on Shivpuri-Jhansi road, it was about 9.30 p.m. There I found my patrolling party near the lower lake. I asked them if they had seen Collector's jeep going to Jhansi side or any other side. Yes! said they. They had seen a few minutes before only, going towards Shivpuri town. We thaught, they must have taken him to the civil hospital for treatment only, so I rushed to the District Hospital. Even there was no trace of Collector's jeep or the forest guard. Then at last I came to the Kotwali, Shivpuri, where I could find my forest guard with blood stained pyjama and also Sardar Hira Singh of Neemdhana, almost in same condition. The S.O. was recording the statements. The injury on forest guard was not very serious. When I asked about the Collector, they said that he had gone to the 'Mela'. When I reached Mela, Mr. Rajan was having Sugarcane juice. He told me "*Aao Sharma sahib, woh sardar ko hamne thikane laga diya*". "I said that he was real quick and thanked him also."

Actually the forest guard first rang up to Collector and then for me at D.F.O. Shivpuri's residence. The Collector thinking that I might take some time in arranging staff, he came to the ongoing mela straight, took police force already posted there with him and then to the forest guard. They did not want this Sardar to run away after attacking the Government servant. Mr. Rajan asked the forest guard if he knew the residence and the village of the accused. He said, yes! it was Hira Singh of Neemdhana village. They drove straight to Neemdhana village on Jhansi road and to the house of Hira Singh. His wife said that Hira Singh was not at home. He had actually hidden himself in the field behind his house. The police force brought him out and then was given the right treatment and then brought to the police station. F.G. Karan Singh had actually caught Hira Singh's cattle illicitly grazing in the park, a few days back and just to take revenge, he assaulted him.

Similarly, once at 6.30 p.m., I had just come back from fire site in the park after fighting it for about four hours, when Mr. Rajan came to my residence and said that there was fire in the park on left side of the Jhansi road. Actually he was then returning from Jhansi and noticed this fire, which was not very big. There is a forest nursery on the other side of the road and some staff is always available over there. I said "O.K., don't worry I will go there immediately and see to it." He said, "Shall I send the fire tender from Municipal Corporation?" I told him that it was not required, as forest fires are not extinguished by fire tenders, we will have to beat it out. Then he left. I came to the Range Office, gathered some staff and labour and then to the nursery. I was astonished to see our Collector, Mr. Rajan in his jeep near Bhadaian Kund and a fire tender following him. He said, "I also came with this fire tender, but your boys are very smart, those 4-5 boys in the nursery only extinguished it before our arrival".

In yet another incidence, my Range Officer was returning with the confiscated buffaloes, illicitly grazing in side the park, which belonged to a very notorious village. It was middle of the park and mid-night. Suddenly they felt that they were surrounded by the villagers. Our staff stopped and hid themselves behind rocks. Now the villagers started pelting stones on them. After some time, the range Officer Asked the forest guard to fire in the air to scare the villagers away. He did so twice. There was a lull for some time. Then this foolish forest guard said loudly to the Range Officer that they had exhausted the cartridges. This thing was heard by the villagers also, in the silence of the mid-night. So they started a fresh attack on our staff. With great difficulty, they saved their own lives and came back to the H.Q., but the buffaloes were taken back by the villagers. Next day when I told Mr. Rajan about the incidence, he said, "why did they fire in the air? They should have fired on the chest. What business did those rascals have to enter the park in the middle of the night. After all I would have come to enquire into this matter".

This was our Collector, Mr. Rajan, whom I will always cherish in my memories.

Episode-XXIX

SPs Who Always Helped, Whenever in Need

In Panna National Park, the northern boundary is formed by Panna-Chhatarpur state highway from Ken river upto Pandav fall chowki. Thereafter, it crosses the road further north for about three kilometres. Thereat the beginning at Ken river is a small village of Madla, a police station also. Here at Madla, Mr. Lokendra Singh, ex-Rajkumar of Panna is having an agriculture farm, just adjacent to the Park boundary. Further adjacent to it was an abandoned 'Kothi' or bungalow of another brother of Mr. Lokendra Singh. Once police from Panna found that some automobile thieves were using this abandoned bungalow as a hiding place and also used to change the number plates and colours of the stolen vehicles. Police recovered a few vehicles also from this spot.

One day on 6-4-90, I had come back from my office. The time was about 7.00 p.m., the wireless operator brought a message from Mr. Chauhan, Range Officer, Madla that one red coloured jeep was standing hidden behind the abandoned Gata chowki, on Chhatarpur road. Nobody was there in the jeep and it had no number plate also. R.O. requested me to come immediately, envisaging some poachers, who might have gone inside the park also. My driver had gone home. Immediately I rang up to Mr. Vivek Johri, the S.P. Panna and requested him for some help. He sent one sub-inspector and two armed constable, within five minutes to my residence. I took them along and drove my gypsy myself, straight to the spot. Just beyond Pandav fall chowki, on Panna-Chhatarpur road, there is a small culvert. One jeep was standing on this culvert facing towards Chhatarpur only. It was quite dark and as I crossed over, we noticed that this jeep was also red in colour and without any number. Mr. Manvendra Singh and his son only were sitting in it and apparently were waiting for somebody. The sub-Inspector, who was sitting beside me, asked me "*Yeh wohi gaadi to nahin hai*?" (this may not be the same jeep). I said how can this be, the R.O. and the other staff are already on the spot. I preferred to go about a hundred metres ahead at Gata chowki and confirm it. I never thought that the Maharajkumar of Panna can do any mischief. Our talk was overheard by Mr. Manvendra Singh. When we reached the spot, the Range Officer and the other staff were there on the spot along with many other people, who were passing on the road.

On my asking, he said "Yes! It was Mr. Manvendra Singh and his son, who had gone inside with two guns. When they returned there was no dead animal with them. I asked them as to why did they enter the park with weapons, they said they had gone to one village for some work." The R.O. had asked them to wait for my arrival and tried to stop them by standing in front of their jeep (the other staff was scared and they left him alone and kept standing very far from them – fear and the influence of royal family). But Manvendra Singh sat in his jeep and drove away with his son, forcing his jeep as if dashing against the R.O. He saved himself at the last moment by moving on one side. As they were telling me all about this, there was some noice in the darkness, just inside the rubble wall of the park. About four to five persons were trying to lift a dead Wild Boar and keep it on the wall. We all rushed towards them, they left the boar there itself and vanished in the dark. It was a huge Wild Boar, shot and then entrails removed. I immediately sat in my gypsy with Sub-Inspector and police constables and drove back to catch Mr. Manvendra Singh, who perhaps was waiting for these men with the Wild Boar. We did not find him on that culvert, where he was standing that time. We came to Pandav fall chowki, the guards there informed us that Manvendra Singh had just crossed that chowki towards Panna at full speed. I followed him to catch up, but could not do it up to Panna. He was going very fast. Now instead of going to his palace, I went straight to S.P.'s bungalow. When I told him as to what had happened, he asked me if the bullet was there in the dead body of the Wild Boar. I said, "I did not see the entire body thoroughly in the torch light and can't say anything". Then S.P. asked me to go and confirm it again and in the meantime, he would look after Mr. Manvendra Singh.

I again returned to Gata chowki with S.O. Madla. Here at Panna, S.P. sent the same S.I. on motor cycle to the palace and called Mr. Manvendra Singh to his residence. When S.I. reached the palace, Manvendra Singh, his wife and son, after locking the jeep in a garage sat in a fiat car and came out of palace. Again driving very fast. The S.I tried to stop him but he did not. The S.I. turned his motor cycle again towards S.P's. bungalow. S.P. also had come out in his jeep following that S.I., envisaging that Manvendra Singh would not come easily. When S.P. came to know that Manvendra Singh was trying to run away, he asked the S.I. to overtake his car and get the barrier on Satna road closed. Even he started following him. It was all in a filmy style. Hardly two hundred metres from the barrier, S.I. over took his car, got the barrier locked and started waiting for both Manvendra Singh's car and S.P's. jeep. He had to stop the car. When S.P. reached there he sent S.I. to call Manvendra Singh from his car. Instead of Manvendra Singh, his son came out of car and then to S.P. When S.P. asked him as to from where were they coming and where were they going. He replied, "we have been invited at a dinner at Devendra Nagar, we are going there and we are coming from the palace only." S.P. asked, "you have done poaching in the National Park". He said, "no, we never went to the park today" S.P. said, "the forest department has sent a complaint that one forest guard was hit by your bullet and he is in the hospital in a serious condition." "On hearing this, this fellow ran back to his father and told him all about their talks. Now came Manvendra Singh with sweat on his fore head and said, "Well, Sir! We had gone to the park but never shot at the forest guard, how can he be injured by my bullet". That was sufficient for the S.P. to take action. He asked both the father and the son to sit in his jeep and asked driver to drive Manvendra Singh's wife back to the palace in his car.

Back here at Gata chowki, when I saw the dead body second time, I could not find any bullet in it. Actually below neck, the entire part of the abdomen along with alimentary canal had been cut and thrown in the park itself. There was every possibility that the bullet also must have been thrown with that soft portion of abdomen. Now I asked them, where might that had been shot. R.O. said that there was a water hole (a big tank) about one and a half kilometre inside, they must have shot it there only. I took 2 – 3 persons with me and left for the tank on foot. I was afraid that it might not have been taken away by the scavengers like jackals. We reached there in about half an hour and searched around. In the dark night, it was very difficult to search such a thing in the light of torches only. Our hard work gave us success and we found the entire thing intact, wrapped in Palash leaves. We returned to Gata chowki and then to police station, Madla along with R.O., Station Officer, the dead body of the Wild Boar, and tried to find out other clues. in the light of electricity. Up to 10.30. p.m., when there was no information from Panna, I decided to return. I was driving alone in my gypsy back, when near Gata chowki again I came across S.P's. jeep coming from Panna. I stopped my gypsy, S.P., Mr. Johri said, "*Aiye Sharma Sahib, hum unhe le aaye hain.*" (Come on Mr. Sharma, I have brought them along with me.) When I got down, Mr. Johri introduced myself to Mr. Manvendra Singh, who in turn said, "I am Raja bahadur Manvendra Singh". I said, "Yes, I know, we met twice earlier also, once when you came to my residence at Umaria with your wife, I was Director, Bandhavgarh National Park, then. Second time, myself and Mr. Hasan, the then Director, B.N.P. were sitting at Tala, after the departure of our P.M. Mr. Rajiv Gandhi, you came and met us there and this is our third meeting. "Yes, Yes! Now I remember" was his reply.

Well! We came back again to Madla Police Station. Mr. Johri told him clearly to tell us the truth, so that the matter is not complicated much. But they were not accepting that they had shot that Wild Boar. Again they were repeating the same thing of going to Budhrod for some work. Weapons they had carried for their self defence. Anyway, at about 1.00 a.m., S.P. asked me to return to Panna, leaving them there only. As we got up from the chairs, Manvendra Singh also got up, S.P. asked him to keep sitting there only and that only myself and the S.P. were returning back. Then Mr. Manvendra Singh asked, "Till when we will have to sit here?" S.P. said, "Till this Station Officer and the Range Officer want you to be here." And we came back. The S.P. had asked S.O. to bring only son to seize the gun used in Shikar from the palace in the morning and not the father.

But what happened between the S.O. and Manvendra Singh in the night, that he brought both of them to the palace in the morning. Once they entered the palace, none of them came out with the gun. S.P was very much annoyed on that S.O. Now he asked him to seize that red coloured jeep and bring it to the police lines. In that also, the S.O. was making lame excuses. Ultimately, S.O was given ultimatum to seize by 4.00 p.m. or not to return to his Police Station, instead get attached to the police lines. Then only, the red jeep was seized for the first time. A lot of hue and cry was there in the town.

Next day we got the shikar kit of Manvendra Singh near that tank, with knife and his name written on the bag. The gun was also seized by S.P. and a case was registered against Manvendra Singh under Wildlife Protection Act, 1978 and Arms Act. Mr. Lokendra Singh, the younger brother of the accused was M.P that time. Even he returned from Delhi and met me and enquired everything in details. He said, *"Maine bhai sahib ko kai baar manah kiya hai, mante hi nahin. Ab katghare mein khade ho kar jawab denge to pata chalega."*

The Range Officer, Mr. Chauhan was transferred to Tikamgarh as some 'goondas' were put after him. Later on prosecution was started by police department. And in July–August, I was also transferred as DFO, Raigarh Production Division. After a few years of prosecution in the court, perhaps nothing happened, as all witnesses became hostile. Mr. Johri, S.P. was also transferred immediately, after this case was registered.

In continuation of this case, once I got a phone call from Mr. Lokendra Singh, saying that some poachers jeep is coming tonight from Kanpur and will be doing shikar around Madla, so do some thing. On that day only, I had recovered from five days sickness and was getting ready for the farewell dinner at Officers club for the outgoing Collector, Mr. C.P. Bhargava. I said "O.K. I will see what can I do now." He said, "If you are not doing anything, I will do something". I said, "well! You are welcome to do whatever you like, I will certainly do, whatever is possible for me". I came to the club and told Dr. M.C. Sharma, D.F.O., North Panna about the phone call. Actually, Madla is the boundary for the park and the North Division., so the so-called shikar was possible in the jurisdiction of anybody. He said, "well! It is already 9.30 p.m. now, if anybody has to do poaching, must have done by now. So we send our Range Officer in my jeep and find out if any such chance is there. Madla was only 20 kilometres away and by the time we finish with the dinner, the R.O. could bring back the actual position at Madla. Then, if needed, we could also go to Madla." Well, the dinner was over and it was 12.00 mid-night and the R.O. had not come back. We were a bit worried now. When the Collector was boarding his car after the function, I told Sharma, D.F.O. to inform S.P. and Collector about this phone call, etc. The Collector was curious to know, we said "we will sort it out with S.P. only" (then the new S.P. was Mr. Ashok Dohare, an equally efficient and a dashing officer). Then we told all story to him also. Mr. Dohare was very eager to help us and said, "May be that R.O. has come back and is waiting at your residence. Check it up and if he is not there, inform me at my residence, I will be ready and accompanying you to Madla.

When we came back home, the R.O. was not there. We informed S.P. and were just coming out of our residence, when two persons came on motorcycle and informed D.F.O. that some timber thieves were going to cut some teak trees in a village on Hinauta road and that they will carry the timber in a jeep only, so do some thing. Well! now our priorities were a little different. We came to S.P's. bungalow and informed everything. In my gypsy, joined our third D.F.O., Mr. R.C. Raiger and one Deputy Collector. Mr. Raiger's jeep was to follow us. At S.P's. bungalow, he informed his A.S.P. also to follow us with more force. He also informed him to check up at that village for timber thieves. Mr. Dohare S.P. wanted to drive my new gypsy himself and sat in my gypsy, along with other officers. My driver sat in the jeep which was following us. Mr. Dohare drove very fast and the other jeep could not keep pace with us. Then suddenly, he asked D.F.O. Mr. M.C. Sharma, whether he knew the way to that village, where the timber thieves were supposed to be. Yes! He said, it is on Hinauta road, a few kilometres from the diversion. Then S.P. said, O.K., let us check up that first and then we go to Madla. We turned on Hinauta road. About three kilometres further, there was a *kacha* village road turning. Due to rains, the visibility was poor. So, the moment Mr. Sharma asked him to turn on that road, he turned without looking at the ground first. And we were there in a pool of water. Our gypsy was stuck in the muddy water and all our S.P's. efforts to bring it out in forward or reverse action were futile. Now what to do. On this Hinauta road, there is hardly any traffic in the night, so there was no other vehicle to help us. Our D.F.O's. jeep which was following us could not keep pace with us and hence could not know that we had turned left on Hinauta road, so it also went straight to Madla.

Now unless somebody went on foot, either to the main road (three kilometres) or to our barrier on main road (five kilometres), there was no possibility of getting any help. Mr. M.C. Sharma, Mr. Raiger and the Deputy Collector agreed to walk down to the main road and get some aid. In the mean time, myself and S.P kept waiting in the gypsy itself. Hardly half an hour was passed when all of them came back in the same jeep which was following us. It had gone up to Madla and was coming back to take us. The drivers were shouting, "*Saheb jaldi chalo, wahan bahut gadbad ho gaya hai*" (Sir, hurry up a lot of things have happened there). We hurriedly boarded the jeep, leaving drivers to bring back my gypsy to Mandla. The drivers gave only a small hint that there was firing took place at Madla and the R.O. sent by us was at the Police Station, Madla. Who did it and what was the result of firing was not known.

We rushed to Madla. On way, about two kilometres before Madla, we met Mr. Lokendra Singh in his open jeep coming towards Panna. He stopped our jeep, came rushing and peeped inside, enquiring as to where was the Director. He was a bit disturbed on seeing the S.P. and D.F.O. Sharma on the front seat. They told him that Director was also there in the jeep and asked him to follow us to the police station. There at the police station, Madla, D.F.O. Sharma's jeep was standing, also the Range Officer, sent by us earlier. The Station Officer was also there. They informed us that the Range Officer had gone up to the nursery on right side of the road, to check up a glittering light over there. As he was returning after that, it started raining and before his jeep could come on the main road, Mr. Lokendra Singh came from Madla side in his jeep and fired at the D.F.O's. jeep. Luckily the bullet did not hit the jeep. The Range Officer immediately raced his jeep to the police station and informed everything and halted there only. The bullet had hit the ground and a lot of mud splattered on the jeep. We checked the jeep, it was not hit by the bullet anywhere. Now the S.P. Mr. Dohare asked Mr. Lokendra Singh to tell the truth. He was initially refusing to have fired, but after one hour cajoling, he took S.P. on one side and said that he fired alright but by mistake. He thought that this was the same poacher's jeep, which was expected that evening. Due to rains he could not identify the D.F.O's. jeep. It was a mistaken identity, now whatever you want you can do it. The S.P. told us that he was accepting his fault and was sorry for that. The bullet also did not hit anybody. As such, no case also could be registered, as it would be very weak. So, ultimately he was let off. No other poacher was reported that evening.

What was the *modus operandi* of Mr. Lokendra Singh in inviting me at Madla in the garb of poacher's jeep and then himself firing at the D.F.O's. jeep, only he knows better. But this was an experience in itself, where both the S.Ps. Mr.Vivek Johri and Mr. Ashok Dohare co-operated fully.

Episode-XXX

An Unknown Victim of a Tigress in Panna National Park

On the morning of 26-7-89, message came from Hinauta that a woman was perhaps killed and eaten by some animal, near Khairayya deserted village on the main road. I rushed immediately and found that on the road side a gunny bag was spread open, as if to sit on it. Also there were some belongings of the victim tied in a saree in the shape of a bundle (*gathri*). When we opened it, some wheat grains, a few clothes and a few utensils were there, nothing else. There was a blood trail going towards the forest compartment No. 526. Even two sarees were all along this trail, as if it got off the body of the victim while it was being dragged into the forest.

About thirty feet distance from her gunny bag was an open land. Then started dense under growth of bushes. The crown of the bushes was very dense due to rains, but underneath, one could see up to quite far distance. So we had to bend ourselves then quietly follow the blood trail. After about two hundred metres, I found a bunch of hair of that unfortunate lady. We were keeping a gun with us and walking very cautiously. It was almost a rocky area with hardly two inches deep soil. Although blood trail was there, we could not find any pug marks. A little further, I could see the skull with some hairs and a few bones. We tried to search for the animal and the other parts of the body, but could not.

The police was informed and all formalities were completed. It was strange that the entire body was eaten by the killer (most probably a tiger and bones by some hyena). Some distance away, the pug marks of a tigress were seen on the road. On further enquiry, it was revealed that this tigress had two small cubs also with her. Secondly, that the victim was very thin, lean and a short structured woman and was only a beggar. She was even sub-normal and had no relatives around. No

Fig. 30.1: 'Gathari', the Only Belonging of the Ill-fated Woman

Fig. 30.2: Dragmark with the Sarees of the Victim, which Came off her Body

Fig. 30.3: The Head and Hair of the Victim in the Forest

Fig. 30.4: The Remains of the Victim as Collected by Police

body knew her name or whereabouts of her relatives. She used to beg from village to village and survive on the alms. One day earlier, she was seen in the Badgadi village.

From the circumstances, it was evident that she was returning to Hinauta in the late evening through this forest road. She must have been tired and at this point thought of taking some rest on the road side. So she spread her gunny bag and must be sitting with her belongings besides her. Maybe she was keeping her head on her knees. At that time only, this tigress must have noticed her. Because the woman was not in a standing position, the tigress could not identify her as a human being and mistook her for some animal only. The tigress must have been very hungry, so she attacked her assuming as a prey animal and ate her completely after killing. Nobody moves on these roads after sunset, so none could detect it till next morning.

This tigress never repeated killing any human being. Even did not attack anybody after this. Apparently, it was a mistaken identity and this poor, unknown woman became the first and the last victim of this tigress. From the sight, one could derive an inference that this poor lady could not even wrap her saree properly and was wearing two sarees at a time, which came off her body, when she was dragged by the animal. Indeed it was a pathetic scene.

Episode-XXXI

A Rare Sight in Panna National Park

In the evening of 6-5-90, myself and Mr. S.B. Lowalekar, the then C.C.F. (Wildlife) were taking a round of Panna National Park. The time was around 6.00 p.m. Suddenly we saw one animal standing in the burnt patch of Compartment No. 526. It was about a dog size but certainly not a dog. Clearly visible in the burnt open patch, also not moving. It also looked at us. For some time we both were trying to identify this animal with tuft of hair on the pointed tips of ears. When it started moving, then we could remember that it was none else than a Caracal. A very rare and threatened animal. We were lucky to sight this rare animal also, but I was sorry that I could not photograph it. There at Shivpuri, my predecessor, Mr. P.K. Naik once had given a photograph of a young Caracal to me. This animal reminded me of that photograph, which is still as a souvenir for me.

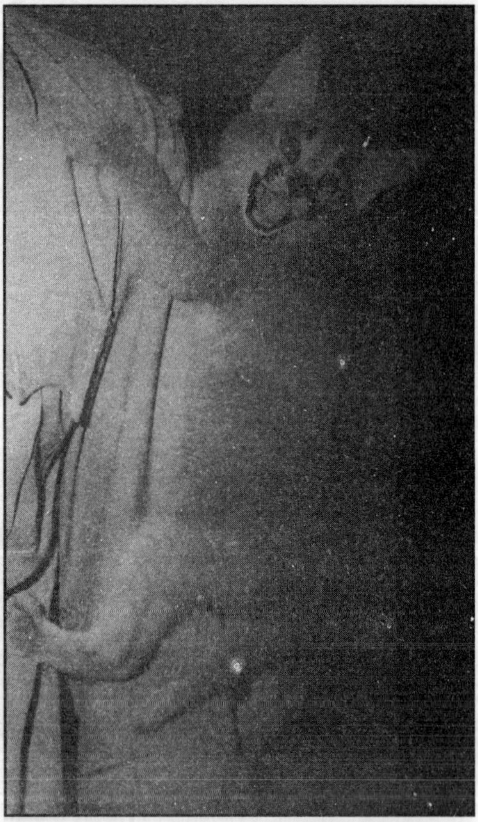

Fig. 31.1: Caracal Cub Clinging to the Arm of a Forest Gurad, Shivpuri

Episode-XXXII

Geharighat, the Beautiful Origin of Ken River

Very few people have seen Geharighat, the origin of Ken river in Panna National Park. During summer it appears like a widespread pool of water, with almost no flow of water in it. But the spot itself is very beautiful, with serenity and its wilderness. From Hinauta it is the interior most place, with no human interference at all. Sometimes the dense jungle on left side becomes an abode of some outlaws/ dacoits only. Otherwise one may not come across anybody over there.

Once I mentioned this beauty to our Collector, Mr. C.P. Bhargava. He showed his willingness to see this spot. I was also planning to show him this place, but we were not getting any suitable dates. Then one day, he gave me a date to go. When I talked with my Range Officer, Hinauta, then he revealed that the then dacoit Charliraja was taking shelter in the forest on that side and a day earlier, kept forest guard of Jhalar beat sitting near him whole day in the village of Jhalar. I was now a bit reluctant to take the Collector with me. It was risky, one never knows how this dacoit may react or behave on finding Collector, right in the deep forest. So, I talked with my S.P. who also asked me not to take risk unnecessarily. He said that he would talk to Collector and make him understand. So the visit was shelved.

But then one day after a few months, our Collector was transferred from Panna. Then again on one day he said, "*Sharma Sahib meri atma yahin Geharighat mein bhatakti rahegi, agar mujhe nahin dikhaoge*" (Mr. Sharma, my soul will remain hear at Geharighat, if you don't show it to me). Now I decided to go once again. The rains had already started. I talked with my new S.P. Mr. Ashok Dohare, beside coming with us, he sent a force of 1–4 persons with us for safety reasons. Even the movement of dacoit Charliraja was not known at that time. When we reached at Geharighat, it was swollen with flood waters. There appeared a number of water falls, some

Fig. 32.1: Geharighat the Origin of Ken River of Panna

Fig. 32.2: Gorge of Ken River, Panna N.P.

Fig. 32.3: Officers Enjoying the Scenic Beauty of Geharighat

shallow and some very deep. What a beauty. Everybody was happy and thrilled. One Bank Officer was also with us, along with his family. Suddenly, I found that this gentleman and his small son were in their under wears. The boy was tied with a long rope in his waist and he was taking bath under a fall. His father was holding the rope. They were taking bath sticking to the wall of the fall (avoiding the main flow of water). Before I could stop them and call them back, our Collector, Mr. Bhargava was also in his under wear and under the fall.

Oh! no. Then I called Mr. Bhargava and requested him not to take unnecessary risk. I reminded him of his own words and said that in reality his soul may not start living there only and his words may not become true. Then he came out along with others. We all enjoyed the scenic beauty of this spot. While coming back, our Collector was lucky to have seen a huge tiger crossing the road in front of his jeep. Panna National Park is full of water falls and it is a sight to look at in peak rainy season. Of course, it is closed to the tourists at that time.

Episode-XXXIII

The Wild Elephants of Surguja

Yes, we know that Surguja district of Chhattisgarh (earlier in M.P.) never had wild elephants for the last about two hundred years from now. But then suddenly in 1988-89, a few appeared in the forests of this district. Actually they were the elephants from the Saranda forest of Tholkabad (then Bihar), who had to leave their homes due to large scale clearance of forest by the activists of Jharkhand Mukti Morcha. There was large scale mining operations also in this home land of elephants, which polluted almost all of the water holes for these poor animals. These elephants had no choice than to migrate into adjoining areas, in search of new homes. There were three such herds, one entered West Bengal, one Orissa area and the last herd entered M.P.

In Surguja district, the forest adjoining the state boundary is segregated in small patches and bears nothing but the monolithic Sal forest. This Sal is also pollarded one. So there was almost no fodder species in these forests for the elephants to feed on. These small patches of forests are scattered and surrounded by various tribal villages.

On 1-12-1988, I was asked by my C.C.F.(W.L.) to proceed immediately to Surguja and beat these elephants out of the state boundary, back to Bihar. I was Director, Panna National Park and had no earlier experience with wild elephants. I had not seen or worked in this Surguja district also, so did not know the geography or the terrain also. Anyway, I came straight to Ambikapur (H.Q. of Surguja) via. Shahdol and contacted the Conservator and D.F.O., North Surguja. By then these elephants had damaged crops/homes in many villages and even killed a few people. I collected the map of the terrain (only majmuli map), that time the topographical maps were not available with the D.F.O. One S.D.O. was asked to accompany me. So we came and halted at Kusumi.

Fig. 33.1: Elephant Herd in the Hill behind Sanna Nursery

Fig. 33.2: Night Camp Fire in Surguja Village to Scare Away the Wild Elephants

Fig. 33.3: Villagers Following the Wild Elephants after Putting Forest on Fire

Fig. 33.4: Full Herd of Wild Elephants on the Run, Surguja District

Next morning, we came to a place called Sanna, a beautiful, undulating country. The main herd of the elephants was supposed to be resting in the forest uphill, behind the nursery of the forest department. The Diwali festival was over but still we could get a few 'Sutali Bombs', the crackers which explode with a loud sound from Sanna market only. By about 12.00 noon, we were just in front of the elephants herd. There was a flat opening between our patch of forest and the one in which the elephants were standing, resting in the shade. The distance between us was about 30-40 feet. They were not disturbed by our presence. We brought the crackers in the centre of that open patch and ignited one. It exploded with a big bang. But I was astonished to find that there was no reaction in the elephants. What of moving away or running away, they did not move even ear or the tail. We repeated the exercise 4-5 times more, but to no avail. Perhaps, these elephants were accustomed to these crackers, which might have been used in all these villages during 'Diwali' festival, hardly a month earlier. We used drum beating also but there was no effect on these elephants. What else could be used to drive them out. This point was about 100 kilometres away from Bihar border.

There was no continuity of the forest up to the state boundary. The elephants were not afraid of human beings, had no fear of crackers or drum/tin beating. They are no cattle, where stones or sticks could be used.

I came back and surveyed the area up to Jashpur, discussed with forest officers of various ranks and then came back to Panna. These elephants were 18 in number. Two herds of 14, 03 and one single tusker. They used to spend whole day in the forest and come out in the paddy fields at dusk time. Graze the crop if it is there sufficient to feed them or else enter the village, search for the house where paddy was stored. Break open the tiled roof or the mud wall of that room where grains were stored. Eat the stored grains. At times, they were getting a chance to drink mahua liquor, kept in the earthen pots also. It was then a feast for them. They were normally not harming human beings, unless interrupted or stopped by them. In the beginning, when they came to the villages, people started offering coconuts, jaggery, etc. and worship them as elephant God coming to their villages. Slowly their damages became enormous and a few human lives were also lost. So the things worsened. As per my experience and discussions with various people, I sent my report that these elephants cannot be driven by any means and will settle down in due course of time.

Again in the month of March, 1989, I was sent to Raigarh and Surguja Districts to study the fresh movement of wild elephants and to propose the mitigation measures. This time, Mr. S.M. Hasan, Dy. C.F. (W.L.), Bhopal was also supposed to accompany me. At Surguja we came to know that it was the same herd of elephants, which had gone back to Bihar and now come back again, entering the Jashpur sub-division of Raigarh district. Also that this time, people (the villagers) were not letting them enter their fields. On the contrary, they were driving these elephants by burning the forest and leaf litter behind them. We asked the then D.F.O., North Surguja to give us toposheets of the area, but to our astonishment he or his office did not have even one. Without toposheets, one cannot have any idea of the terrain of the elephants movement. Anyway, whatever blue prints of Majmuli maps we could have, we took and proceeded to the area of elephant location. On 2-4-89, we reached the forest near village Ramsama of Jashpur Division. We were shocked to see whole lot of people, men, women, girls and boys in hundreds, chasing the elephants. They (the villagers of Bachhraon) were burning the forest behind those elephants and were moving behind them, almost on their heels. They were not listening to any body and were making these elephants run continuously in one direction. When we tried to stop some school going girls, not to follow, lest they would turn back and kill them, they said laughingly, "no, if they come back we will offer them a '*matki*' (an earthen pot of liquor), they will drink it and go back." In the night the elephants occupied an area near a tank of village Sahidand and the villagers remained awake with fire around their houses for safety. On 3-4-89 the elephants moved towards Borpani via Kohpani village. Near Kohpani we tried to feed the herd with artificial feed of Ficus leaves, Gur and some rice. Three elephants from the herd fed on some rice and Gur but the public, who were not encouraging this step and were making a lot of noise, the elephants left and moved ahead towards Bagicha.

Next day on 4-4-89, near Bagicha, when we were observing this drama, Collector, Raigarh District, Mr. Rai also reached there. Even when he asked one person as to since when he was chasing these elephants, he said three days. Then he asked him, where was his village, he said, "about twenty kilometres back". Then the Collector asked him, why was he unnecessarily harassing these, they have already crossed by his village far back. He even scolded him. That day elephants took refuge in thick forest near Bagicha and we could stop this chase by those villagers. We discussed the situation with Collector, Raigarh and other officers. Next two days I surveyed the area of Semarsot sanctuary and also discussed with Field Director Palamau Tiger Reserve of Bihar. Although Semarsot sanctuary formed a good habitat for the elephants, but it didn't have a large area or continuity with other forest area for the elephants seasonal migration. The Field Director Palamau agreed to accept this herd of about fourteen elephants in Palamau, if it could be driven up to this reserve. On the basis of our study and discussions, a report was prepared with a map showing movement routes of three rounds of these elephants.

Actually, they were still searching for a new home to settle down. In this pursuit, they were going back to Bihar, where people used to harass and send them to M.P. again. Now chasing started here also. This was evident that they had no suitable forest area to settle down either in M.P. or in Bihar. Therefore, we proposed only two solutions, one to chase them in this manner right up to the area of Palamau Tiger Reserve, which was far away and involved a lot of risk to human life and property. Secondly, take permission from Central Government and catch the entire herd, tame and use in the parks. This second option was really more feasible.

When we came to Bhopal and submitted the report to the then P.C.C.F. (Mr. V.B. Saharia), he was annoyed to see the Majmuli maps with it. We told him that the D.F.O. Surguja didn't have the toposheets and was not aware of any such maps. He was furious on us and the D.F.O. and asked us to call him immediately to Bhopal to meet him. Well! That was not our job. There at Bhopal, I purchased toposheets from Survey of India office and we prepared another report on it and re-submitted.

The third time, I was working as D.F.O., Raigarh (Production). I was appointed as Zonal Officer in the Parliament Elections of June 9. Suddenly I got a message to proceed immediately to Jashpur and stop the wild elephants from entering M.P., till elections were over. Even C.F. Bilaspur (Mr. N.S. Chaudhary) asked the then P.C.C.F. as to what would Sharma alone do to stop the elephants. But he said, "Nothing doing, just ask him to go. Get him exempted from election duty, it is an order from the C.M." When I met the Collector for exemption from election duty, even he asked, "why only you and what will you do?" I said, "Though I am working as D.F.O. (Production), I am a trained wild lifer. What will I do, even I cannot say with out going to the spot and facing those elephants". Well with great reluctance, he exempted me. I rushed to Jashpur and then straight to D.F.O., Gumla (Bihar). He and his entire staff were also on election duty and he was about to leave his H.Q. I said, "First tell me, where are your elephants, I am supposed to check them from entering our state". He called his A.C.F. and R.O. and enquired from them. They said that the elephants were in the forest of Gangeda, about thirty kilometres away from M.P. border. Secondly, they will not leave that forest area for another 5-7 days as one of the females is about to deliver a calf and no elephant will leave her till she is relieved. Another point that they were even otherwise on their movement towards Ranchi (i.e. away from M.P.). So I was relieved but not satisfied. They all left on election duty. I came back to Jashpur, took a reconnaissance of bordering villages of M.P. Did not find any report of elephants from anywhere. Then in the night, I gave my jeep to two of my Range Officers from timber depot (who were free from election duty) and asked them to go and check the presence of elephants in forest area of Bihar, where the A.C.F. and the R.O. of Gumla were telling them to be. My R.Os. returned in the mid-night and informed me that they had actually seen the elephants at the spot, as said by the Bihar staff and that they were stationary over there. Now I was satisfied.

Next day (on election day) also, I kept on moving along the border all along Bihar state, enquiring about any sighting of even individual elephant. Luckily, no elephant was reported from anywhere. That is how successfully I could stop the elephants from entering in M.P. But till today I am thinking as to what would have happened, had they entered our state and was it possible for me to stop them single handed. The entire Government machinery was busy in holding elections, entire public was busy in voting. Then who would have come and helped me. Only God helps in such cases, where our top leaders and bosses pass such orders without listening to a subordinate officer or even themselves giving a serious thought to the situation.

Episode-XXXIV

The Visit of Your Beloved Leader

In our country there have been so many leaders but a very few leaders are there, who are loved and liked by all. One such leader was our late Prime Minister, Mr. Rajiv Gandhi. When I was Director, Madhav National Park, Shivpuri, he came there to lay the foundation stone for the Tourist Village. That time he was not the Prime Minister, he was only an M.P. But everybody was thrilled to have seen him so closely. It was a short visit and was limited to the site of tourist village only.

Then in March 1985, when I was Deputy Director, Kanha Tiger reserve again for a second term, Mr. Rajiv Gandhi came to Kanha with his family and friends. This time he was our Prime Minister and his team included Mrs. Sonia Gandhi, Ms. Priyanka Gandhi, Mr. Rahul Gandhi, Mr. Arun Singh with his wife, Mr. Brijendra Singh with his wife, Mr. Rajiv Gandhi's brother-in-law and his daughter, family physician, P.As. and the other staff. It was a private visit and the stay was for three nights. The best part of this visit was that none else was permitted inside the park except Park Officials, not even Collector or S.P. It was experience in itself. We worked day and night for a fortnight to make their stay as comfortable as it could be possible. Only park officials and our beloved Rajivji's team. Seeing such a pleasing personality so closely was satisfying experience. We were tensed but not disturbed due to his affectionate and pleasing behaviour with all. As no one else was permitted, there was no official photographer also for the trip. Only myself and Dr. P.C. Kotwal, our Research Officer were having with us two cameras each. In the beginning, we were a little afraid of taking photographs, lest he may not mind it. And first day went without any photograph.

Second day in the afternoon, a tiger was shown to the team near Kisli. After that when everybody sat in his respective vehicle, suddenly all mahauts came to me and requested for a photograph with the P.M. Mr. George was sitting in my jeep. When I told him and asked him if he would mind taking his photograph.

Fig. 34.1: Late Prime Minister Rajiv Gandhi on Elephant Back, Kanha

Fig. 34.2: Late Prime Minister Rajiv Gandhi with Family, Kanha.

Fig. 34.3: Late Prime Minister Rajiv Gandhi with Camera, Kanha

Fig. 34.4: Late Prime Minister Rajiv Gandhi after Tiger Show at Kisli

Fig. 34.5: Priyanka and Rahul Gandhi with Elephants, Kanha

Fig. 34.6: Rajivji at Bandhavgarh

Fig. 34.7: Rajivji and Mrs. Sonia Gandhi on Elephant Back, Bandhavgarh

Fig. 34.8: Mating Tigers, which were Shown to Late Rajivji

He said, "No, not at all. He is our leader and all our leaders are happy when they are photographed". With this he got down and asked Mr. Rajiv Gandhi to come out of his vehicle and pose for the photograph. That was the first photograph by me. Thereafter, we did not miss any opportunity to photograph our beloved Rajivji and his party. The trip was over with a lot of photography by me and Dr. Kotwal. Many tigers, tigresses and the cubs were shown along withal other animals of the park. Everybody was happy and thrilled.

One interesting happening, I still remember. Priyanka, Mrs. Arun Singh, Mrs. Brijendra Singh could not see the Gaurs, during their round of the park. So, one evening, myself and Mr. Lowalekar, F.D.P.T. brought them to Kisli with a hope to find some Gaurs in the evening round. All these three ladies were sitting on one elephant, myself and Mr. Lowalekar were following them on another elephant. Suddenly we noticed that their elephant had a jerky walk and every now and then their 'hauda' cushion was being pushed to the back side and get folded. Then they used to stand on foot board to readjust the cushion. They were very uncomfortable on that elephant. Mr. Lowalekar suggested to exchange our elephants. We got the elephants stand near each other and all three of them came to my elephant. Mr. Lowalekar shifted to their elephant. As that elephant moved again a few steps with big jerks, Mr. Lowalekar was on one corner of the 'hauda' with folded cushion. And all these three women could not stop laughing to look at him in this condition, through which they had been moving for such a long time. Mr. Lowalekar then sat in the centre of the 'hauda' with folded legs and moved his elephant back. Anyway, we could not find any Gaurs that evening and came back to the camp.

Another episode of this trip has been given in episode No. XIX.

Then on 13-7-1985, Mr. Rajiv Gandhi was to come to Bandhavgarh National Park. Mr. S.M. Hasan was Director of the Park. I was asked to move from Kanha with three elephants and a jeep to assist Hasan at Bandhavgarh. I reached three days in advance. Mr. Hasan was busy in discussions with various level officials in preparations for the visit. He was worried that no tiger was located for the last 3-4 days. But on the third day I located one pair of tigers near Jamunia in early courtship. I was sure that they would continue to remain together at least for two more days. I put our elephants on continuous watch, barring a few hours in the night. As the luck would have it, we could show our leader the mating tigers in Bandhavgarh. It was late evening, when he reached Tala and straight away went to the site to see our tigers. I remember him calling my elephant and asking me to take the photographs of these mating tigers with flash gun. I told him, it was dangerous to flash at such a close distance, but I had already taken many photographs during the day time. I had prepared an album of his visit to Bandhavgarh, which I wanted to present to him during his next visit to Kanha or other park of M.P. But unfortunately, he could not come again.

During V.V.I.P's. visits, many funny things happen. During this visit of Bandhavgarh also it happened so. Firstly, Mr. Rajiv Gandhi was supposed to be staying in Maharaja Rewa's 'Kothi' at Tala. Then this being a private building, the stay was shifted to the white tiger lodge of M.P.S.T.D.C. A team from Delhi came and rejected it on security grounds. Now it was decided for the Forest Rest House Tala only. Those who have seen it, know that the rooms are very small of 10′×10′ size only. The then M.D., M.P.S.T.D.C. had asked Mr. Hasan that Mr. Rajiv Gandhi needed seven feet long beds to sleep. So he went to Jabalpur and fetched special seven feet long pair of beds with specially made mattresses, linen and all. Now the time left for his visit was only a few days and all the four suites of Forest Rest House could not be upgraded simultaneously. So only one suite in which Mr. Gandhi was to stay could be done with. A secretary from M.P. Government sitting at Tala was not able to decide as to which room be given for P.M. Another thing, whether A.Cs. were to be fitted or not. Meeting after meeting, but no decision was being taken. Four A.Cs. had come to Umaria but last minute decision was not to fit it due to mainly two reasons. Firstly, that rooms were too small, secondly, the fitting procedure would dismantle the windows, etc. and there was no time enough to do that. The doors of the dressing room and the bath-room were hardly five feet tall and had to be changed. The new paint on new doors could not dry completely. Another problem of paint and distemper smell, one engineer suggested Mr. Hasan to keep crushed onion in a big bowl in the center of the room for whole night with fan on. That would reduce the smell of paint and distemper. But what about the onion smell then. Any way we did not take that risk.

When after the tiger show, Mr. Rajiv Gandhi came to occupy their suite in the forest rest house, Mrs. Sonia Gandhi was shocked to see the small, stuffy room of 10′×10′ size. It was already full with 7′×6′ size of beds, a small table and two chairs. A small ceiling fan, was trying its best to satisfy you psychologically. On realizing the situation, Mrs. Gandhi called for a small table fan to be put under the beds for circulation of air, opened the doors and windows and slept like that only. So we had to put an emergency screen in the verandah for them to be at ease.

But ignoring our unavoidable shortcomings, both went happy from the Bandhavgarh National Park. I cherish all these three visits in my memories and am proud to have seen that smiling face so closely through my camera.

Episode-XXXV

The Child Lifter of Bamhanwada

The people in rural M.P. are still very simple. Their main source of entertainment is chanting *'Kirtan'*, singing and dancing during festivals, marriages, attending weekly markets and enjoying the *'Ram Katha and Ram lila'*. Sometimes they walk 20-30 kilometres distance and keep awake till late in the night while attending such *'Ramlilas'*.

On 07-10-92, about twelve persons of village Barbaspur in Chhapara range of North Seoni division were returning back to their village after seeing a Ramlila at Lakhanadon. They were walking almost in a single row on a footpath, which passed near forest compartment No.762 RF., between Bhimgarh and Barbaspur.Also there was a plantation of 1990 in this coupe No. I of compartment No. 762. The time was around 4.00 a.m., so most of them were quite sleepy also. A small girl Sant Kumari d/o Dhullu Bhoi of Barbaspur, aged about 11 years was walking between Janaki (16 years) and Manak Ram (19 years). Suddenly near a bush they realized that Sant Kumari was missing. Then in the darkness they could only see that she was being dragged by some animal towards the hill top. These two started shouting for help. Then all of these villagers gathered but had no lights or torches with them. Before they could decide to follow the animal, it had gone quite far with its catch. They were a bit afraid also to follow without light. So they waited till the day break and then moved in a group in the approximate direction. There on the top of the hillock was a small temple, a kilometre distance from the site of attack. A few steps further, they found the dead body of that unfortunate girl. The body was eaten near thigh and the chest. On hearing the villagers approaching it, the animal left stealthily. Nobody saw the animal. I was informed at Seoni, where I was working as Conservator of Forest Seoni Circle at that time.

By the time I reached the spot, it was late evening. Due to movement of many people by that time, the pug marks were obliterated and not clear anywhere. But

Fig. 35.1: The Child Lifter Leopard Trapped Successfully, Seoni

the way she was caught near a bush and soon lifted and dragged over a long distance indicated it to be a leopard only. I got one drop shutter cage set near the temple and came to Chhapra. It was really pity to see the dead body of that small girl, who became a victim with no fault of hers. After the post-mortem, she was cremated there at Chhapra only, on the bank of river Banganga. The compensation was paid as per rules.

During enquiry, I could know two more incidences in the surrounding villages in the near past. On 02-03-92, Gangai wife of Phoolmat aged 65 years was injured in the field, while she was working there. In another incident, on 18-6-92, Dallan Bai d/o Komal Singh, aged 8 years was dragged up to 50′ in the courtyard of her house, but was saved by the villagers. The animal left her and ran away. The animal was striking at an interval of 2-3 months. Probably was not totally invalid in hunting, otherwise the frequency would have been still shorter. That indicated that it was surviving on normal kills and was intermittantly trying its hand on human beings also (children), when it was very hungry for some days. So we had to be cautious. There was no news of the animal around the trap cage. I asked the D.F.O. to notify the villagers to avoid walking near the forest in the night and that too alone.

On 29-12-92, I was informed that another child Mahesh Kumar s/o Basant Kumar Pardhan, aged 13 years was killed in the village Bamhanwada. I came rushing to the village and was told that the ill fated child was sleeping with his *'Nana'* (maternal grandfather) in the field. They were sleeping under a *'Chhatri'* (a thatch roofed umbrella) and keeping a watch of the crop. His grandfather Lekhan Das had lighted a small fire also near them, as it was quite cold in the night. Whole night he was keeping his hand on his grandson Mahesh. Suddenly, at about 2.30 a.m., he also fell asleep and turned his back. After some time as he again wanted to put his hand on the child, he was not there. He woke up with a jerk and saw with his wide open eyes that the child was being carried away by an animal towards *nala*. For a few moments he was spell-bound and did not know what to do. Then suddenly he rushed after it, shouting in a panic. But by that time that animal had vanished in the dark bushes of the *nala*. In about ten minutes, other villagers also gathered and then followed that direction for some distance, but could not find either the child or the animal. They abandoned the search due to darkness of night and fear of the animal.

Next morning, the dead body of the ill fated child Mahesh was found in the bushes on the bank of Bijana *nadi*. It was also about one-third eaten. About half a kilometre from the field of Lekhan Das, one footpath was leading to the Bijana *nadi*. On the slopes of this footpath, just before the river was the bush, where the dead body was found. I decided to fix the trap cage on the river bed near this foot-path with a dog as a bait. All of the villagers around this spot were notified to keep vigilant and careful, not to keep children alone, especially in the night and also to inform the nearest forest chowki to report sighting of any leopard in that area. For two days there was no success. But I continued our trap cage at that very spot. During enquiry it was revealed that a man by name Amarlal of Semartal had seen a leopard near Bijana *nadi* at about 3.00 p.m. on 29-12-92. The leopard growled at him, then he climbed a tree and remained atop for about one hour. He got down only when the leopard left that spot. That night, this leopard caught a dog near forest chowki of Semartal, but on hearing the shrieks of the dog people came out and could get the dog free from the clutches of leopard. That very night, this leopard lifted Mahesh Kumar in Bamhanwada.

On 4-1-93, I got the good news that the culprit leopard was ultimately trapped in the cage and our patience proved fruitful. We were lucky that the menace was controlled in a short time and after only two children having become its victim. I came to Bamhanwada and brought the leopard to Seoni. It was a big male leopard, absolutely fine in health except that its one eye was white and opaque. Only one eye was O.K. and could not see anything with the other one. This was the reason, why it started picking up children, when it used to be very hungry. The interval of attack on human beings was longer, that showed that it must have been able to kill some small animals like dogs occasionally.

Such white opaque eyes are generally caused due to some injuries in the wild. It may be caused accidentally while capturing wild animals from its horns or while passing through some thorny bushes. One such blind leopard was caught from a hut in Mandla district and brought to Kanha by Mr. S.B. Lowalekar. It was nick named as 'Soor Das', because it had lost both the eyes. Its blindness was checked by me by releasing a live cock inside its cage. The leopard was not looking at it but on hearing its movement sounds was following it and trying to capture it by imagining the position of neck and other parts. Our Veterinary Doctor was not sure of any surgery or treatment of its eyes. So it remained in Kanha for over one year in perfect health. It never injured itself like other cats, because was not seeing human beings coming to its cage. It used to get agitated on hissing sound made by our lips. A peculiar reaction, may be it used to find some similarity with the hissing sound of snakes/cobra.

Episode-XXXVI

A Leopard in the Well, Saved Well

On 6th February, 1990, I was on my way to Bhopal from Panna. At Sagar, when I reached at 3.30 p.m., I went to our C.F., Sagar Circle to pay my regards and inform him that I was going to Bhopal to meet my Chief Wild Life Warden. On seeing me, he appeared greatly relieved, as if he was waiting for me only. Our C.F., Mr. R.D. Sharma immediately said, "It is good that you have come, now go to D.F.O., Sagar, one tiger has fallen in a well in a village near here, go and take it out." I was taken aback by this proposal, because I was never prepared for it. Secondly, I had no equipment with me to handle a tiger. What could I have done bare handed. But my argument did not serve any purpose. He said that all Commissioner, Collector and the local leaders are worried, so I had to go to that village and do some thing. Then I came to D.F.O's. office. One S.D.O. was there, who had returned from the spot and was quietly doing his routine work. He told me that it was not a tiger, but a leopard, which was alive and quite hale and hearty.

First I fired him and asked him as to why did he not inform the C.F. till now that it was a leopard and not a tiger. Because both are having different structures, habits and requirements and so have to be dealt with in a different way. Then I informed C.F. accordingly and that I was going straight to the spot and do my best to solve the problem. Myself and the S.D.O. reached the village (Badnawar) at about 5.30 p.m. Sun was about to set, but there was sufficient light to see everything in the well. This well of about 20′ diameter was about 30′ deep and had no parapet wall around it. It was located on one corner of the field of a farmer. A few small bushes here and there and a few small trees of *Zizyphus* and Guava were also planted in a row near the well.

A lot of people were still surrounding the well, peeping inside and making a lot of noise over there. The leopard was sitting on a small rock which was protruding out of water. The water in the well was not very deep, hardly 2–3′

deep. I tried to remove the mob from there, but it was real hard task. I had to do something before it was dark. I enquired from the farmer and others who were seeing this animal since morning, whether it could move from the rock or not. They told me that it was jumping up to 5 to 6′ height, when was being disturbed or teased by people up to noon. Only now it was a little docile and calm. Obviously, it was tired. Now it was clear that it had all the four legs good and uninjured due to fall. Apparently also no other injury was visible from the top. Second thing that I had to check hurriedly was its eyesight. It was to be sure that it was not blind when it fell into the well. I called for a live cock from the village, along with 30 to 40′ long thin rope (*sutali*). I tied two legs of the cock at one end of the rope and hanged it inside the well, deep enough to dangle it over the head of the leopard. Yes! Our leopard was smartly looking at the cock moving from one end of the well to the other. At times, it tried to have a paw on it also. It was confirmed that it had no problem with the eyesight also.

Now I thought of bringing it out and releasing it again there *in situ*. But how? A wild tiger being very heavy in structure, may not try to climb on a straight bamboo ladder, but a leopard which climbs straight trees easily, will leave no chance unattempted if ladder is given to it. So I called for bamboo ladders, which were available in that small village. The ladders were small, hardly 5-6′ long, which was unsuitable for a 35′ deep well. With great difficulty eight ladders were collected and rope also to tie them together. Then tying ladder by ladder lowered it in to the well. The leopard was also looking at us with curiosity and trying to make out our intentions. By about 9.30 p.m., we could reach the bottom of the well. The top ladder also was about one foot above the well. Now I made every- body to move away from the well, so that no human voice was heard by thc leopard. Myself, S.D.O., Range Officer and a few other people took position at a hide about 30′ away, keeping our eyes on the well. It was a dark night and we could hardly see anything, but certainly we could sense any movement of our leopard near the well. We waited till 10.30 p.m., then S.D.O. brought me back to Sagar for dinner. The Range Officer was asked to wait there only till it came out. He was asked to check the well again only after another one hour and not earlier. I promised to come back again if there was any further problem or I was called anytime. After dinner I was made to stay in a hotel at Sagar Cantt. only.

In the early next morning, the Range Officer came with a good news that the leopard had gone out of the well, within half an hour of my departure from the village site. I immediately rushed to the village again to confirm it before people and the cattle could disturb and de-face its pug marks. The leopard had gone in the direction of the adjoining forest, perhaps from which it had come to the well. We could see its pug marks of almost running speed. Then asked the farmer, "Sir you have released it again over here only, if it comes back and troubles us again?" My reply was, "This leopard must have not looked back once, up to two kilometres from here, what of coming back. It also must be abusing you, thinking what type of ditches you have dug up in this area. It will never return in this area again, at least in your field, so do not worry".

So this is how we can handle some situations without any equipment. The problem was solved within a few hours time. Only then I was realizing my mistake of refusing on the first instance to handle this without any equipment or kit. Howsoever urgent was for me to reach Bhopal, it was not urgent than this leopards release from the well. Had I refused to come to Badnawar then, our C.F. would have called another team from Kanha or elsewhere, who would have done the same thing after another 12–14 hours time. We should never take any decision without going to the spot in such emergencies. Our priorities can save a lot of money, time, labour and lives too. Then I would have missed that hospitality of S.D.O. with a good dinner and a nice stay in a good hotel. It was indeed a well-saved leopard with a very little effort.

Episode-XXXVII

Some Administrative Problems

I started working with the wildlife wing of M.P. from 1977-78, the time when wildlife started getting some importance for the first time. Till then, only Kanha National Park was known for wildlife in this state. The other National Parks and Sanctuaries were just for the name sake. Excepting Kanha, all were deficient in staff and the funds. Even at the centre, hardly any funds were allotted for wildlife.

Thank God that the Project Tiger had already been started. Whatever budget was being given, was for these prime areas. In M.P. the then Forest Secretaries, Mr. Samar Singh and Mr. M.K. Ranjit Sinh were two persons, who were and are still working for wildlife. It is during their period that wildlife wing got many more areas added as Sanctuaries or National Parks. Almost all potentially good areas were included in the wildlife wing.

This was one part of the wing expansion. But the most important part, posting of the managers and the lower functionaries was good and under control, till Mr. Ranjit Sinh and Mr. J.J. Dutta were there as Forest Secretary and the Chief Wildlife Warden, respectively. Later on the conditions kept on deteriorating, which were even otherwise never up to the mark. One aspect was 'willingness' of the staff to work in the wildlife wing. It is said that nobody is willing to work in the wildlife wing. Even during the period of Mr. J.J. Dutta as C.W.L.W., the officers used to say that they were ready to work, till Mr. Dutta was there as C.W.L.W. The situation was very unfortunate. People after getting wildlife training also used to shirk working in this wing. In my opinion, the reasons why these officers were not ready to work in this wing are:

1. It is a specialized job while dealing with wild animals.
2. A limited jurisdiction, as compared to regular Divisions of the Forest Department.

3. The works are more in wilderness than in public areas, taste differs.
4. Where there is tourism also, have to devote much of the time for the visitors, V.I.Ps. and V.V.I.Ps. Therefore no time for own children and families.
5. The H.Qs. are comparatively at very small places, and are lacking educational and medical facilities.

And the reasons for other lower staff are:

1. It is a specialized job.
2. Smaller jurisdiction as compared to territorial units.
3. Have to work mostly in wilderness areas (no human populations around), a monotonous atmosphere.
4. More promotional aspects in the territorial units than in wildlife. A very important aspect.
5. More taxing as more and more importance is being given to wildlife wing by public and the media.

When new National Parks and Sanctuaries were created, there were two types of field staff for such units. The first were those, who were acquired *in situ* with the units, when they were carved out from the territorial units. The others were those, who were appointed on new additional posts sanctioned under the wildlife wing. There used to be a funny discrepancy in such units, the staff newly appointed such as Game Guards, Game Supervisors, were getting a token special pay for working in wildlife wing, whereas those who joined the unit *in situ* were deprived of getting this special pay. Why? The job was same, responsibility was same and the unit was same. For many years, this difference prevailed so also the 'heart burn' amongst the staff.

These few are the reasons, why people do not want to work in the wildlife wing. When I was Principal, Forest Rangers College, Balaghat, Mr. Rajesh Gopal, the then Field Director, Kanha asked me to find out some Ranger trainees, willing to work in wildlife (especially in Kanha) and I was astonished to see that none of the new Rangers was willing to go to the wildlife wing, even the one who was topping in Wildlife Management subject and was awarded a gold medal. Way back in 1981, when I was Director, Bandhavgarh National Park, I was having one Ranger working against sanctioned posts of four. I met the Consevator, Shahdol circle. He appeared quite willing and eager to post one more Ranger from the Special Duty Rangers. I wanted one young, direct Ranger, especially for the Forest Rest House duty, because many V.I.Ps. had started coming to this park and a smart F.R at the reception was urgently needed. C.F. got the list and asked me to name the person. I said, "I don't know anybody, whom shall I name?" But on his insisting again, I named the first person on the list of nine. He said O.K. and called his clerk to issue orders. I came back to Umaria. Next day, got a phone call from C.F., saying,

"Sorry, that F.R. has been given to D.F.O., North Shahdol, I am giving you the third one". I accepted that even. D.F.O. South, Mr. Pathak said, "I am sending this Ranger to you, but he is a useless worker" I said, "the beggars have no choice, I will try to take work from him only." So this new Ranger was posted at the Forest Rest House, giving a quarter adjacent to it as his residence.

One day the then Dy. C.C.F. Mr. S.N. Bhosle was on his way to Umaria from Rewa. It was late evening of winter, when his vehicle broke about one kilometre after crossing the F.R.H., Tala. He left his car there, came to the F.R.H. and decided to stay there over night. After dinner, when he went to sleep, he wanted an additional blanket. The F.R. had gone to his residence by that time and the keys to the box were with him only. When R.H. attendant came to his residence, our F.R. had gone to sleep, as his father informed the attendant. When he asked him to wake him up as the Dy. C.C.F wanted an additional blanket, his father replied, "no, now nobody is supposed to wake him up, we cannot disturb him". So, our Dy. C.C.F. had to sleep with only one blanket that night. Next morning he fired him and was furious even at Umaria. This Ranger was transferred back. Then next C.F., Shahdol (Mr. N.K. Joshi) was requested. He used to ask me, "come with the written consent of any Ranger to work in your National Park, I will post him." What was this? Was it my personal National Park, why should I go and beg from person to person to give his consent. It was really a very unfortunate situation.

Actually, the postings in the National Parks and Sanctuaries are governed by the Territorial Conservators of Forest, who in turn post only those staff who are rejected by their Territorial D.F.Os. All sick, mischievous, weak, absconders, drunkards, useless old Forest Guards/Foresters are posted in Wildlife units. A rare exception may be there like in Kanha, which has got some saying up to some time C.M./P.C.C.F. level, the other units suffer very badly. Sometimes one may succeed in getting some good staff posted but then either the orders are cancelled before implementation or they are again transferred out after a short stay in the wing.

The things are really bad for wildlife. There was a time, when orders were issued that the postings into and out of wildlife wing would not be done, unless the persons were approved by the Chief Wildlife Warden. The Territorial Conservators took it otherwise, as if somebody was interfering on their birth right. When I was Director, Shivpuri National Park, C.F., Gwalior Circle called all D.F.Os. including me with transfer proposals. During meeting, he discussed with all D.F.Os. and in the last after three hours said to me, *"Arey, aap to wildlife wale ho, aap log apna dekh lena kya karna hai"* (Oh, you are from wildlife wing, you may see yourself what to do) and he closed the meeting. He did not even listen a word about National Park. A step-motherly treatment.

Even when World Bank's India Eco-development Project was going on in Pench National Park, during one appraisal meeting, it was agreed by the department to fill up 22 Forest Guards posts, which were vacant in a stipulated time. Yes! It was done, posting orders were issued but hardly 2-3 joined, the rest of the orders were cancelled one by one. Most unfortunate thing. Whenever the V.I.Ps., V.V.I.Ps., various level committees come to the state, they are taken to the National Parks only. All of the families and friends of ministers, secretaries and other forest officers would like to go and enjoy in these very National Parks, but whenever staff or funds are asked for, they turn a blind eye. Why? The Wildlife wing has become well equipped and richer, due to thanks to the World Bank Projects, otherwise, the State Government did not have even salaries to pay to the staff. Once I asked my Forest Minister as to why these National Parks were being spoiled by giving rotten staff to us. I had to give him a simily for this, I said, "Consider this Forest Department as a big house and different wings as rooms in it. Whenever some guests come they are made to sit in the drawing room and we keep our drawing room furnished with best of our furnishings, neat and clean. Whosoever comes as a guest to Forest Department, he is taken to Kanha, Bandhavgarh and other Parks only, in other words to our drawing rooms. And how have we furnished these, with all rejected, invalid and useless staff (furniture). He smiled and said, "What to do, nobody wants to come to the wildlife". Now what can we do if the Government itself is feeling helpless.

Another point that the number of posts sanctioned for these parks and the sanctuaries are very old. As the works have increased many folds with increase in development works and the tourism, it needs to be revised and sufficient staff has to be posted to run these units satisfactorily. The grassroots level staff, i.e. forest guards and the foresters have to be increased as per actual requirement. A number of forester circles and the beats are vacant due to paucity of staff. One forest guard is looking after 2-3 beats at a time. The same staff is looking after other development works and the tourism, thereby the protection work suffers badly. The capacity of a man cannot be doubled, working whole day on development and other works and then patrolling in the nights for protection sake, cannot be done all the time.

At the time of promotions also, generally the forest guards and the foresters posted in National Parks and the Sanctuaries are neglected. A forest guard gets promotion to the post of forester, only if he is confirmed at the post of forest guard. The confirmed forest guard posts are allotted by the territorial C.Fs., to various N.Ps. and the Divisions. And the confirmed posts in the National Parks are so few as compared to the regular Divisions, that some of the forest guards in N.Ps. do not get confirmed even where as their batch-mates and even juniors get promotion to the post of forester in a regular Division, much early. Who would like to come to the wildlife wing then. One forest guard, Mr. Bhuwan Bhaskar Pande, joined Bandhavgarh National Park in 70s and is still a forest guard. And is about to retire in a couple of years. What a pity, working in wildlife wing and this punishment. Who will rectify all these things? The wildlife wing is a part of same forest department, but the treatment given to the officers and the lower staff by the regular wing officers and the staff is not at all co-operative.

If you compare even the office staff, the Field Director of a Tiger reserve is a conservator level and his office does not have even thirty per cent staff, as that of a regular Conservator circle. That too, all rejected accountants, U.D.Cs., L.D.Cs., even peons and the drivers are given to the wildlife wing. Why? These days a number of informations are required to be submitted even by the Field Director's office at a very short notice, but with such a rejected staff F.D.P.T. has to struggle for days to compile and send with help of this rejected staff. O.K., less staff can manage the things better, if their quality is good, but here the worst of the whole lot is given to this wing.

I remember one incidence. There at Delhi, in one of the National level meeting, there was discussion going on pug mark census method of tigers/panthers. The reliability was being questioned. It was accepted that if properly traced a pugmark, compared and analyzed sincerely, this was the most reliable method till now. Then Director, Dudwa National Park, U.P. said that more than fifty per cent of his staff were old and were having such a poor sight that they were unable to see the pug mark under a tracer, leave alone tracing it. So even in other states also the conditions do not appear to be very satisfactory.

Now with the conditions described as above, how do we expect to save the tigers and leopards and even other wildlife. Only Field Director, Deputy Directors and a few other gazetted officers alone cannot protect the precious wildlife. They need healthy and able hands to do it. Otherwise, we will just be blaming each other and find some lame excuses for their extinction in near future.

All said and done, if we really feel that a tiger is very important animal and it has to be saved at any cost. Spare such statements that if tiger also becomes extinct what difference will it make, human beings are dieing with hunger and you are talking about the safety and protection of these wild animals. Such people cannot think in positive for tigers and other wildlife. We should ignore such people, they will never understand the theory of survival of tigers, means survival of man. So keeping in view the controversy of tiger population and its poaching in various National Parks, the following are a few suggestions:

I. *Allotment of staff*:

(a) A proper number of staff be allotted, as per actual requirement. Wherever tourism, eco-development and other such activities are going on, special staff should be posted for such activities. The protection staff should be spared from doing other works.

(b) The young and the able staff to be posted in wildlife units. How? Once selected and posted, no cancellation/change be permitted under any circumstances. No political pressure be accepted. The Government has to be firm in it or else the wildlife wing tenure may be made compulsory for all, say five years tenure between the age of 30-40 years. Without that, no further promotion in the forest department be given to anybody.

Making the Territorial Conservators also the Field Directors of the Tiger Reserves will change the scenario. Then he will have to bear the responsibility of tigers and the wildlife also and will post proper staff in such units also.

(c) Transfer within the wildlife wing, right up to the forest guard level should be free of all restrictions. Local people Forest Guards/foresters get themselves near their home towns/villages, with the political approach. Then they do not move from there, whether they work or not. Secondly, they are under pressures from local *shikaries*/poachers, who are either far related or known to them or are so influential that these forest guards are scared of them. Sometimes they may even join hands with them. Therefore, a separate policy should be made for the wildlife staff.

(d) The wildlife wing should be made immune to the pressures from different unions of staff, hoteliers, guides, etc.

(II) *Rules to be made more stringent*:

(a) If we really want to save the tiger from the hands of human beings, we have to give full protection to it. Grazing in all tiger areas to be stopped completely. No. entry of human beings to be permitted, at least in the Project Tiger areas. And then such areas should be protected on the same lines, as those for all military installations in the country. Any unauthorized entrant should be shot down. In a democratic set up of our country it may look cruel and barbarous, but we have to do it, if we want to protect our tigers.

(b) These days a number of tigers are being electrocuted through the high tension lines, which are supplying power to the rural areas around the protected areas. It should be made obligatory for all Electricity Boards to insulate all such lines or make them under ground, around all P.As.

(c) We know that the nomadic tribe, the '*Bahelias*' are doing most of the poaching in all our National Parks and Sanctuaries, with the help of 'Gin traps' and poisoning. They are a few hundred families, busy mainly in poaching only. They have got nucleus at Katni and operational area all over M.P. and other states. Why not to take care of these families through some N.G.Os. Put the Entire families on some job to subsist, educate them and take their help in conservation, instead of destruction. It may work.

Recently, the Government of India has proposed an 'Adivasi bill', which will relax almost all restrictions in the forest for the Adivasies or the tribals. Some social workers are advocating the old system of co-existance of tribals and the wildlife. They are still living in that old era, when the tribals used to live in the most remote areas with hardly any requirements. They were not in touch with the modern day living and the physical needs of a modern Indian. That time they were in real sense the Friends of Forest. But certainly not now. The corrupt man from all over has reached these innocent people, polluted their mind also. Now they also want to acquire everything. Yes! They also do have a right to everything but not the resources. The urge to acquire everything, will force them to cut the forest, sell timber and the wildlife which is there around them. Even otherwise, I have seen these tribals cutting big trees just to get one rat or a cocoon of Kosa. Burning big chunks of forest during *Parad* or the community hunting, and then killing each and every animal that comes their way. Such rituals are still going on many areas. So in a sense they cannot be called as the so called 'Friends of Forest' any more. Giving them right on the lands of Reserve Forest and the wildlife areas will be disastrous for forest, wildlife and the whole environment. In other words, disastrous for human beings of this country. If still they pass such a bill, then they should stop talking about the Tiger and its survival.

Index